The International Labour Organization (ILO)

The International Labour Organization (ILO) is broadening its agenda and carving out a role as a key player in global economic policy-making, and this volume provides a succinct and comprehensive guide to this important organization.

By charting the history and development of the ILO and examining its key functions and structure, the authors offer a clear and detailed account of its work, and provide an important discussion of the current criticisms and debates that surround the organization. The work moves on to discuss the position that the ILO takes in our understanding of global governance and seeks to evaluate the impact of emerging issues such as the global economic crisis, and critically examines the future direction of the organization.

This fresh and accessible account of the International Labour Organization provides an excellent understanding of its purpose and structure and will be of interest to all students of international politics, international organizations, and international political economy.

Steve Hughes is Professor of International Organisations and Director of Accreditation Strategy at Newcastle University, UK.

Nigel Haworth is Professor of Human Resource Development at the University of Auckland Business School, New Zealand.

Routledge Global Institutions
Edited by Thomas G. Weiss
The CUNY Graduate Center, New York, USA
and Rorden Wilkinson
University of Manchester, UK

About the series

The "Global Institutions Series" is designed to provide readers with comprehensive, accessible, and informative guides to the history, structure, and activities of key international organizations as well as books that deal with topics of key importance in contemporary global governance. Every volume stands on its own as a thorough and insightful treatment of a particular topic, but the series as a whole contributes to a coherent and complementary portrait of the phenomenon of global institutions at the dawn of the millennium.

Books are written by recognized experts, conform to a similar structure, and cover a range of themes and debates common to the series. These areas of shared concern include the general purpose and rationale for organizations, developments over time, membership, structure, decision-making procedures, and key functions. Moreover, current debates are placed in historical perspective alongside informed analysis and critique. Each book also contains an annotated bibliography and guide to electronic information as well as any annexes appropriate to the subject matter at hand.

The volumes currently published are:

45 The International Labour Organization
Coming in from the Cold (2010)
by Steve Hughes (Newcastle University) and Nigel Haworth (University of Auckland)

44 Global Poverty
How Global Governance Is Failing the Poor (2010)
by David Hulme (University of Manchester)

43 Global Governance, Poverty, and Inequality (2010)
Edited by Jennifer Clapp (University of Waterloo) and Rorden Wilkinson (University of Manchester)

42 **Multilateral Counter-Terrorism (2010)**
The global politics of cooperation and contestation
by Peter Romaniuk (John Jay College of Criminal Justice, CUNY)

41 **Governing Climate Change (2010)**
by Harriet Bulkeley (Durham University) and Peter Newell (University of East Anglia)

40 **The UN Secretary-General and Secretariat (2010)**
Second edition
by Leon Gordenker (Princeton University)

39 **Preventive Human Rights Strategies (2010)**
by Bertrand G. Ramcharan (Geneva Graduate Institute of International and Development Studies)

38 **African Economic Institutions (2010)**
by Kwame Akonor (Seton Hall University)

37 **Global Institutions and the HIV/AIDS Epidemic (2010)**
Responding to an international crisis
by Franklyn Lisk (University of Warwick)

36 **Regional Security (2010)**
The capacity of international organizations
by Rodrigo Tavares (United Nations University)

35 **The Organisation for Economic Co-operation and Development (2009)**
by Richard Woodward (University of Hull)

34 **Transnational Organized Crime (2009)**
by Frank Madsen (University of Cambridge)

33 **The United Nations and Human Rights (2009)**
A guide for a new era, second edition
by Julie A. Mertus (American University)

32 **The International Organization for Standardization (ISO) (2009)**
Global governance through voluntary consensus
by Craig N. Murphy (Wellesley College) and JoAnne Yates (Massachusetts Institute of Technology)

31 **Shaping the Humanitarian World (2009)**
by Peter Walker (Tufts University) and Daniel G. Maxwell (Tufts University)

30 **Global Food and Agricultural Institutions (2009)**
by John Shaw

29 **Institutions of the Global South (2009)**
   by Jacqueline Anne Braveboy-Wagner (City College of New York, CUNY)

28 **International Judicial Institutions (2009)**
   The architecture of international justice at home and abroad
   by Richard J. Goldstone (Retired Justice of the Constitutional Court of South Africa) and Adam M. Smith (Harvard University)

27 **The International Olympic Committee and the Olympic System (2009)**
   The governance of world sport
   by Jean-Loup Chappelet (IDHEAP Swiss Graduate School of Public Administration) and Brenda Kübler-Mabbott

26 **The World Health Organization (2009)**
   by Kelley Lee (London School of Hygiene and Tropical Medicine)

25 **Internet Governance (2009)**
   The new frontier of global institutions
   by John Mathiason (Syracuse University)

24 **Institutions of the Asia-Pacific (2009)**
   ASEAN, APEC, and beyond
   by Mark Beeson (University of Birmingham)

23 **UNHCR (2008)**
   The politics and practice of refugee protection into the twenty-first century
   by Gil Loescher (University of Oxford), Alexander Betts (University of Oxford), and James Milner (University of Toronto)

22 **Contemporary Human Rights Ideas (2008)**
   by Bertrand G. Ramcharan (Geneva Graduate Institute of International and Development Studies)

21 **The World Bank (2008)**
   From reconstruction to development to equity
   by Katherine Marshall (Georgetown University)

20 **The European Union (2008)**
   by Clive Archer (Manchester Metropolitan University)

19 **The African Union (2008)**
   Challenges of globalization, security, and governance
   by Samuel M. Makinda (Murdoch University) and Wafula Okumu (McMaster University)

18 **Commonwealth (2008)**
Inter- and non-state contributions to global governance
by Timothy M. Shaw (Royal Roads University)

17 **The World Trade Organization (2007)**
Law, economics, and politics
by Bernard M. Hoekman (World Bank) and Petros C. Mavroidis (Columbia University)

16 **A Crisis of Global Institutions? (2007)**
Multilateralism and international security
by Edward Newman (University of Birmingham)

15 **United Nations Conference on Trade and Development (UNCTAD) (2007)**
by Ian Taylor (University of St. Andrews) and Karen Smith (University of Stellenbosch)

14 **The Organization for Security and Co-operation in Europe (2007)**
by David J. Galbreath (University of Aberdeen)

13 **The International Committee of the Red Cross (2007)**
A neutral humanitarian actor
by David P. Forsythe (University of Nebraska) and Barbara Ann Rieffer-Flanagan (Central Washington University)

12 **The World Economic Forum (2007)**
A multi-stakeholder approach to global governance
by Geoffrey Allen Pigman (Bennington College)

11 **The Group of 7/8 (2007)**
by Hugo Dobson (University of Sheffield)

10 **The International Monetary Fund (2007)**
Politics of conditional lending
by James Raymond Vreeland (Georgetown University)

9 **The North Atlantic Treaty Organization (2007)**
The enduring alliance
by Julian Lindley-French (Center for Applied Policy, University of Munich)

8 **The World Intellectual Property Organization (2006)**
Resurgence and the development agenda
by Chris May (University of the West of England)

7 **The UN Security Council (2006)**
Practice and promise
by Edward C. Luck (Columbia University)

6 **Global Environmental Institutions (2006)**
by Elizabeth R. DeSombre *(Wellesley College)*

5 **Internal Displacement (2006)**
Conceptualization and its consequences
by Thomas G. Weiss *(The CUNY Graduate Center)* and David A. Korn

4 **The UN General Assembly (2005)**
by M. J. Peterson *(University of Massachusetts, Amherst)*

3 **United Nations Global Conferences (2005)**
by Michael G. Schechter *(Michigan State University)*

2 **The UN Secretary-General and Secretariat (2005)**
by Leon Gordenker *(Princeton University)*

1 **The United Nations and Human Rights (2005)**
A guide for a new era
by Julie A. Mertus *(American University)*

Books currently under contract include:

The Regional Development Banks
Lending with a regional flavor
by Jonathan R. Strand *(University of Nevada)*

Peacebuilding
From concept to commission
by Robert Jenkins *(The CUNY Graduate Center)*

Non-Governmental Organizations in Global Politics
by Peter Willetts *(City University, London)*

Human Security
by Don Hubert *(University of Ottawa)*

UNESCO
by J. P. Singh *(Georgetown University)*

Millennium Development Goals (MDGs)
For a people-centered development agenda?
by Sakiko Fukada-Parr *(The New School)*

UNICEF
by Richard Jolly *(University of Sussex)*

The Organization of American States (OAS)
by Mônica Herz (Insitute of International Relations, Catholic University, Rio de Janeiro)

FIFA
by Alan Tomlinson (University of Brighton)

International Law, International Relations, and Global Governance
by Charlotte Ku (University of Illinois, College of Law)

Humanitarianism Contested
by Michael Barnett (University of Minnesota) and Thomas G. Weiss (The CUNY Graduate Center)

Forum on China-Africa Cooperation (FOCAC)
by Ian Taylor (University of St. Andrews)

The Bank for International Settlements
The politics of global financial supervision in the age of high finance
by Kevin Ozgercin (SUNY College at Old Westbury)

International Migration
by Khalid Koser (Geneva Centre for Security Policy)

Global Health Governance
by Sophie Harman (City University, London)

Think Tanks
by James McGann (University of Pennsylvania) and Mary Johnstone Louis (University of Oxford)

The Council of Europe
by Martyn Bond (University of London)

The United Nations Development Programme (UNDP)
by Stephen Browne (The International Trade Centre, Geneva)

Religious Institutions and Global Politics
by Katherine Marshall (Georgetown University)

South Asian Association for Regional Cooperation (SAARC)
by Lawrence Saez (University of London)

The International Trade Centre
by Stephen Browne (The Future of the UN Development System (FUNDS) Project, Geneva) and Samuel Laird (University of Nottingham)

The Group of Twenty (G20)
by Andrew F. Cooper (Centre for International Governance Innovation, Ontario) and Ramesh Thakur (Balsillie School of International Affairs, Ontario)

The UN Human Rights Council
by Bertrand G. Ramcharan (Geneva Graduate Institute of International and Development Studies)

The International Monetary Fund
Politics of conditional lending, second edition
by James Raymond Vreeland (Georgetown University)

The UN Global Compact
By Catia Gregoratti (Lund University)

For further information regarding the series, please contact:

Craig Fowlie, Senior Publisher, Politics & International Studies
Taylor & Francis
2 Park Square, Milton Park, Abingdon
Oxon OX14 4RN, UK

+44 (0)207 842 2057 Tel
+44 (0)207 842 2302 Fax

Craig.Fowlie@tandf.co.uk
www.routledge.com

The International Labour Organization (ILO)
Coming in from the cold

Steve Hughes and Nigel Haworth

Routledge
Taylor & Francis Group

LONDON AND NEW YORK

First published 2011
by Routledge
2 Park Square, Milton Park, Abingdon, Oxon, OX14 4RN
Simultaneously published in the USA and Canada
by Routledge
270 Madison Avenue, New York, NY 10016

Routledge is an imprint of the Taylor & Francis Group, an informa business

© 2011 Steve Hughes and Nigel Haworth

Typeset in Times New Roman by
Taylor & Francis Books
Printed and bound in Great Britain by
CPI Antony Rowe, Chippenham, Wiltshire

All rights reserved. No part of this book may be reprinted or reproduced or utilized in any form or by any electronic, mechanical, or other means, now known or hereafter invented, including photocopying and recording, or in any information storage or retrieval system, without permission in writing from the publishers.

British Library Cataloguing in Publication Data
A catalogue record for this book is available from the British Library

Library of Congress Cataloging in Publication Data
Hughes, Stephen, 1955–
  The International Labour Organization (ILO): coming in from the cold / Steve Hughes and Nigel Haworth.
     p. cm. – (Routledge global institutions ; 45)
     1. International Labour Organization. I. Haworth, Nigel. II. Title.
  HD7801.H85 2010
  344.01–dc22
                         2010015661

ISBN 978-0-415-35382-3 (hbk)
ISBN 978-0-415-35383-0 (pbk)
ISBN 978-0-203-34764-5 (ebk)

Library
University of Texas
at San Antonio

In memory of Maureen Ann Hughes and for Edward Henry Hughes, and for Robert and Sylvia, Cal and Ru and the "tight four."

Contents

List of illustrations		xiv
Foreword		xv
List of abbreviations and acronyms		xix
	Introduction	1
1	A brief history of the ILO	5
2	Structure and organization of the ILO	20
3	The ILO and globalization	33
4	The Declaration on Fundamental Principles and Rights at Work: a new approach to labor standards?	46
5	The ILO and the WTO: the tortuous case of the Social Clause	61
6	Decent Work, Fair Globalisation and strategic planning: Somavia's ILO	73
7	The ILO at work in the 2007 global economic crisis	85
8	Concluding thoughts: whither the ILO?	95
	Select bibliography	104
	Notes	106
	Index	115

Illustrations

Table

1.1 Directors-general of the ILO   6

Figures

2.1 International Labour Office senior management structure   22
6.1 Relationships between the strategic objectives   76

Box

2.1 Eight fundamental or "core" conventions contained in the Declaration on Fundamental Principles and Rights at Work, 1998   25

Foreword

The current volume is the forty-fifth in what has now become recognized as a dynamic and well regarded series on "global institutions." The series strives to provide readers with definitive guides to the most visible aspects of what we know as "global governance" as well as forensic accounts of the issues and debates in which they are embroiled. Remarkable as it may seem (particularly as the situation has not changed in the half decade since the publication of our first volume), there exist relatively few books that offer in-depth treatments of prominent global bodies, processes and associated issues, much less an entire series of concise and complementary volumes. Those that do exist are either out of date, inaccessible to the non-specialist reader, or seek to develop a specialized understanding of particular aspects of an institution or process rather than offer an overall account of its functioning. Similarly, existing books have often been written in highly technical language or have been crafted "in-house" and are notoriously self-serving and narrow.

The advent of electronic media has helped by making information, documents, and resolutions of international organizations more widely available, but it has also complicated matters. The growing reliance on the Internet and other electronic methods of finding information about key international organizations and processes has served, ironically, to limit the educational materials to which most readers have ready access—namely, books. Public relations documents, raw data, and loosely refereed websites do not make for intelligent analysis. Independent analyses compete with a vast amount of electronically available information, much of which is suspect because of its ideological or self-promoting slant but which is free. Paradoxically then, a growing range of purportedly independent websites offering analyses of the activities of particular organizations has emerged, but one inadvertent consequence has been to frustrate access to basic, authoritative, critical, and well-researched texts. The market for such has actually been reduced by the ready availability of varying quality electronic materials.

For those of us who teach, research, and work in the area, the lack of access to up-to-date and authoritative information has been particularly frustrating. We were delighted when Routledge saw the value of a series that bucks trends and provides key reference points to the most significant global institutions and the evolution of the issues that they face. Routledge knows that serious students and professionals want serious analyses, and they are willing to pay reasonable prices to have that access. We have assembled a first-rate line-up of authors to address that market. Our intention is to provide one-stop shopping for all readers—students (both undergraduate and postgraduate), interested negotiators, diplomats, practitioners from nongovernmental and intergovernmental organizations, and interested parties alike—seeking information about most prominent institutional aspects of global governance.

The International Labour Organization (ILO)

The ILO can be characterized as something of a series of paradoxes among international institutions. Its birth is intimately connected with both a desire to develop an international dimension to the improvement of working conditions and to efforts put in place a robust machinery with which to combat Soviet-style revolution. Despite being almost a century old, the ILO's tripartite decision-making structure (with representatives not only of governments but of employers and employees as well) is among the most forward thinking, inclusive, and representative of all international institutions; yet the organization has very little influence in, and is largely peripheral to, contemporary global economic governance.[1] The ILO has consistently been at the forefront of championing social issues, for which it was awarded the 1969 Nobel Peace Prize on its fiftieth birthday; yet it has been unable to systematically ensure member state compliance with many of its key conventions.[2] Throughout much of its history, the organization was deeply embroiled in, and hamstrung by, superpower politics. Although the institution has evolved incrementally and rather conservatively, year on year adding to its suite of conventions and quietly pushing forward research into new areas and aspects of the world of work, it has consistently been guided by a dynamic succession of executive heads. Likewise, although the history and politics of the ILO are among the most dramatic of all international organizations, the institution is seldom given a mention in debates and discussions about, or courses on, international organization and global governance. And debates about the merits of including non-state actors in the formal decision-making structures of international organizations have largely stalled, leading instead to a growth in international public-private partnerships, exercises in subcontracting, and networked constellations of institutions; yet the ILO's unique tripartite structure offers not only a compelling example of what can be achieved when state and non-state actors are brought together, but also an exercise in democratic accountability few other world bodies can claim.

Given the ILO's relative lack of coverage in the literature on international organizations it is unsurprising that few books exist that offer in-depth accounts of the institution.[3] Moreover, those that do exist are now very dated.[4] And while they offer useful insights into the historical circumstances of the ILO's birth along with the politics and development of its evolution, they provide inadequate guides for the modern reader. But, the relative lack of works dealing with the ILO is surprising for another reason. The ILO has always made very substantial use of academics and researchers (many of whom have been and are prolific writers) in the development of institutional policies, in various research activities, and in the implementation of its programs. Yet very few resembled Robert Cox and analyzed the institution.[5] And no one has yet to subject the ILO to the kind of ethnographic study to which other UN bodies like the Security Council are routinely subjected.[6]

We have long bemoaned the absence of a complete and authoritative account of the ILO; and full length treatment of the organization has been on our "wish-list" since the series was first established. We also knew exactly who should write the book—Nigel Haworth and Steve Hughes. We knew that they would offer a compelling and rigorous treatment of the ILO, and the pages that follow do just that.

Haworth and Hughes—respectively professors of human resource development in the Business School at the University of Auckland, New Zealand and of international organizations in the Business School at the University of Newcastle, UK—bring to the volume the fruits of their long, considered, and acclaimed engagement with international labor issues, the role of the ILO in world politics, and standard setting. Significantly, both are contributors to the ILO's century project, a research project designed by Director-General Juan Somavia to improve knowledge of and about the ILO in advance of the 2019 celebration of the organization's centenary.

What follows is an examination of the ILO that is among the very best and most readable accounts of this fascinating institution that was founded at the same time as the League of Nations and survived that organization's demise to become a specialized agency of the UN system.

We are delighted to have it in the series and we strongly recommend that anyone interested in the politics and political economy of international organizations put this volume high up their list of essential readers. As always, we welcome comments from our readers.

Thomas G. Weiss, The CUNY Graduate Center, New York, USA
Rorden Wilkinson, University of Manchester, UK
March 2010

Abbreviations and acronyms

CSR	Corporate social responsibility
DFID	United Kingdom Department for International Development
DWCP	Decent Work Country Programme
DWPP	Decent Work Pilot Programme
DWT	Decent Work Technical Support Team
ECOSOC	United Nations Economic and Social Council
FDI	Foreign direct investment
GATT	General Agreement on Tariffs and Trade
GNP	Gross national product
GSP	General system of preferences
ICFTU	International Confederation of Free Trade Unions
IDA	International Development Association
IILS	International Institute for Labour Studies
ILO	International Labour Organization
IMF	International Monetary Fund
IPEC	International Programme on the Elimination of Child Labour
ITC	International Training Centre
ITO	International Trade Organization
ITUC	International Trade Union Congress
MDG	Millennium Development Goals
MOPAN	Multilateral Organisation Performance Assessment Network
NAFTA	North American Free Trade Agreement
NAALC	North American Agreement on Labor Cooperation
OECD	Organisation for Economic Cooperation and Development
OPEC	Organization of the Petroleum Exporting Countries
PCI	Policy Coherence Initiative

PRGF	Poverty Reduction and Growth Facility
PRSP	Poverty Reduction Strategy Papers
SPF	Strategic Policy Framework
UNDP	United Nations Development Programme
WEP	World Employment Programme
WTO	World Trade Organization

Introduction

If the post-war Keynesian "golden age" ended sometime in the late 1970s, to be replaced by a new dawn of market liberalism and reduced state regulation, it appears that we have now turned a circle. At the time of writing, the global economic crisis continues apace and the world economy has spiraled into recession. The venality of modern banking practices has found a place in everyday discussion and "toxic assets" continue to drain the coffers of government rescue packages. During April 2009, the G20 held a summit in London, closing with a much trumpeted $1.1 trillion deal that included tripling resources available to the International Monetary Fund (IMF), more support for trade finance and a new financial regulatory environment that involved the setting up of a Financial Stability Board with a remit to extend regulation and oversight to all financial institutions, instruments and markets. Empowered by the recession, governments are back, interventionism is in, and regulation, particularly international regulation, is the new mantra. In a shock to ideological purists and the certainties of late twentieth-century economic liberalism, it appears markets are not self-regulating after all.

It is in this context that our gaze turns to the International Labour Organization (ILO). Before the advent of "sub-prime lending," "toxic assets" and huge bonuses awarded to bankers, the social costs of trade liberalization and the calling for a "fair" globalization had become a central part of ILO activities. Perhaps paradoxically, the changes forged in the 1970s and embedded in state thinking thereafter came to offer more opportunity than threat to an organization that was struggling to retain a role in the changing international system. Instead of being cut adrift and fading into obscurity, the ILO found itself part of a powerful movement calling for a social dimension to the globalization agenda.

A key forum for these concerns turned out to be the World Trade Organization (WTO) which, newly established in 1995 following the conclusion of the General Agreement on Tariffs and Trade (GATT)

Uruguay Round, found itself struggling to contain a growing lobby calling for a "Social Clause" to be attached to multilateral agreements. That Social Clause was based on ILO labor standards. While the often acrimonious Social Clause debate was eventually jettisoned from WTO agendas, it placed a hitherto marginalized ILO back into the center stage of international social policy. Examining the emergence and reinvigoration of the ILO after the Social Clause debate forms a large part of this book, which assesses a growing consensus on the important role the ILO can play in a more integrated and coherent system of global governance. The call by Dominique Strauss Khan, managing director of the International Monetary Fund (IMF) for increased co-operation between the IMF and the ILO in policy co-ordination between multilateral agencies demonstrates the political momentum behind this consensus.[1]

The ILO still has a rocky road ahead in establishing a place for itself at the high table of international policy co-ordination. However, the vision, ambition and political acumen of its current director-general, Juan Somavia, and his predecessor, Michel Hansenne, have played a large part in formulating the ILO agenda into something that is relevant to the times and offers a sustainable platform for national initiatives on employment and social welfare. As we argue in the book, Somavia is the latest in a line of ILO directors-general, who have devised and implemented strategic responses to global social justice and welfare challenges. Before Somavia, Michel Hansenne grasped the opportunity afforded by the Social Clause debate, and the refusal of the WTO to embrace the measure, to lay the foundations for ILO renewal. The roles played by Somavia and Hansenne over the last two decades are an ILO tradition. Each successive director-general, from 1919 to the present day, has left an indelible stamp not only on the operation of the organization, but also on how we perceive the ILO and how the ILO perceives itself.

The ILO has not been immune to the politics that permeate all international organizations. The Cold War structured many of its debates and underpinned controversies that included the temporary withdrawal of the United States in 1977 under the Carter administration. Controversy dogs the organization still. Many of the strategic initiatives introduced in recent years, including the 1998 Declaration on Fundamental Principles and Rights at Work and the Decent Work agenda, have attracted pointed criticism. The ILO has been accused, first, of failing to develop a coherent response to the challenge of structural adjustment and labor market flexibility laid down in the 1980s; second, of sustaining a system of labor rights promotion that is in crisis; and, third, of a future that looks uncertain. Much of this criticism comes from those who are generally supportive of the ILO and have worked closely with it (or indeed in it) but have become concerned about its strategic direction and associated processes and policies. We examine these criticisms and some of the responses in our discussion.

At the heart of ILO activity is its tripartite system of governance (unique in the United Nations), and its long-established focus on the introduction and protection of international labor standards. Its administrative headquarters, the International Labour Office, is housed in Geneva and forms part of a constellation of international organizations located in Switzerland. It works in an imposing building, reflecting the ILO's status and complex administrative functions, as it administers to the needs of its tripartite constituents and also serves as an executive for its extensive global programs. Yet in viewing for the first time the sheer size of its Geneva residence and experiencing the sometimes stifling and rigid bureaucracy at its core, it is often easy to forget the profound contribution the ILO has made to economic thinking and labor protection, a contribution recognized by a Nobel Peace Prize in 1969. The fact that the ILO marked its ninetieth birthday in 2009 is testament to its resilience, the dedication of those who work for it, the quality of its technical advice and support, and the relevance of its role.

We begin in Chapter 1 by examining the historical development of the ILO following its foundation in 1919. We show how the ILO survived the demise of the League of Nations and became a founding organization of the United Nations after the Second World War. We also chart the checkered post-war history of the ILO as the Cold War took its toll on ILO activities. Chapter 2 provides an insight into the ILO's organizational structure and the regulatory processes that govern its standard setting activities. In particular, it explains how the ILO's tripartite structure, in which government, trade union and employer representatives work together, establishes international labor standards. In following chapters, we shift gear and begin our assessment of the contemporary ILO. In Chapter 3, we look at the debate in the ILO around globalization. Globalization, and how the ILO has responded to it, has been the key context for contemporary developments in the organization. In Chapter 4, our focus is the 1998 Declaration of Fundamental Principles and Rights at Work, which explicitly takes up the challenge of globalization. The declaration, a controversial measure, refocused the work of the ILO to meet the challenge posed by globalization. Chapter 5 discusses the unresolved issue of the link between trade and labor standards, which has provoked a major debate about the role of labor standards in globalization. The abortive attempt to embed labor standards to the global trade system triggered a strategic reassessment within the ILO, which is taken up in Chapter 6. Here we examine the Decent Work agenda, which since 1999 has sought to establish the importance of ILO standards in the new global order, and is today the ILO's main strategy. Chapter 7 is a contemporary case-study of the ILO in the context of the global economic downturn, which began in 2007. In Chapter 8, we conclude by assessing the debate around the ILO's renovation after 1994, and indicating the future debates that will surround a renovated ILO.

1 A brief history of the ILO

The idea of an international organization dedicated to developing and regulating international agreements on labor protection arose from a challenging mix of social, political and economic unrest following the end of the First World War. The movement for international labor legislation began gathering momentum when the humanitarian concerns of Victorian and European philanthropists such as Robert Owen and Daniel Le Grand were overtaken by the potential for working-class revolution and the problem of international competition. Faced with the threat of new and aggressive competitors in traditional overseas markets, and the increasing strength of organized labor, which now took a global as well as national dimension with the birth of the first Internationals, state legislators, working with civil society interest groups, began examining ways in which social justice could be promoted. Debate considered the best way to do this, either through international treaty or private agreements between "progressive" manufacturers. The outcome of the debate was support for the development of some form of international agreement, subsequently translated into Part XIII of the Treaty of Versailles 1919 and the birth of the ILO.

The ILO served the political, economic and humanitarian interests of countries desperate for peace following the savagery of the First World War, and its development has been driven by the same mix of interests ever since. The ILO's unique tripartite decision-making apparatus has served it well and helps explain its longevity. In the ILO context, tripartism means a constitutional arrangement in which member states are represented in ILO activities by three parties (government, employers and trade unions). However, if tripartism is a success, the complex bureaucracy that it requires has at times made the ILO a cumbersome and remote organization for the very people it was set up to protect.

In this chapter, we map the history of the ILO, focusing in part on the leadership and activities of successive directors-general, most of

6 *A brief history of the ILO*

whom have played an influential and lasting role in the ILO's development (see Table 1.1). Our starting point is the immediate post-World War I period when the ILO was first led by the Frenchman, Albert Thomas. We develop our analysis through the actions of successive ILO Directors-General up until the recent tenures of Belgium's Michael Hansenne and Chile's Juan Somavia. Here we are necessarily brief as the rest of the book is largely dedicated to the policy initiatives introduced by Hansenne and Somavia.

The struggle for institutional life

Albert Thomas was elected the first director of the ILO on the basis of his knowledge and experience of the working class and the international labor movement. This experience, gleaned from his years as a socialist politician and wartime minister, was in contrast to the British civil service background of his rival for the directorship, Harold Butler.[1] This experience helped him to procure the vote of the Workers' Group and develop an early but clear vision of the ILO's role. For Thomas, the purpose of international discussion on labor issues was to improve legislative protection for labor. This would be achieved not only by understanding better the forms of labor legislation in different countries but also by understanding how these forms were influenced by the impacts of international trade and competition.

For Thomas, a key task for the ILO was to persuade governments, employers and workers alike that there was always an international dimension to the construction of national labor standards, a dimension that drew on a complex mix of humanitarian, political and economic concerns. It was to be understood as a dynamic process requiring dynamic responses. However, Thomas faced some formidable obstacles to realizing his grand vision. Restricted to a strict interpretation of the articles

Table 1.1 Directors-general of the ILO

Director-general	*Country of origin*	*Period in office*
Albert Thomas	France	1919–1932
Harold Butler	United Kingdom	1932–1938
John G. Winant	United States	1939–1941
Edward Phelan	Ireland	1941–1948
David A. Morse	United States	1948–1970
C. Wilfred Jenks	United Kingdom	1970–1973
Francis Blanchard	France	1974–1989
Michel Hansenne	Belgium	1989–1999
Juan Somavia	Chile	1999 to date

of the Paris Peace Treaty, the ILO ran the danger of becoming a bureaucratic institution with no real authority and of diminishing relevance in a world still nervously coming to terms with changes wrought by war and revolution.

The First World War had brought the issue of labor legislation to the forefront of national and international debate. Public opinion, prompted by social and political unrest and the threat of further war, had compelled governments to take up labor issues in their international conferences. Thomas argued that workers of the post-war world wanted two fundamental things: stability in daily life and security against the threat of war. From this, he conceived for the ILO a dual role; first, to lessen the tension *within* nations and, second, to lessen the tension *between* nations. To achieve this, he had to construct an organization that utilized Article XIII of the Treaty to its fullest effect. This involved moving beyond the establishment of humane conditions of work and the collection of information on the condition of labor, to the promotion and establishment of political, economic and moral rights for the individual, a doctrine which Thomas believed could give to the ILO both unity and identity.[2] His was an idealism combined with a cold recognition that a failure to take a proactive approach to fulfilling worker interests would result in the political isolation of the ILO and its abandonment, not only by workers, but also by employers and governments, already skeptical of its role and achievements. For Thomas, the ILO was an organization in which the pursuit of peace through social justice required the projection of worker needs into the realm of international relations.

It was a high risk strategy. For it to succeed it needed two conditions to be fulfilled: the continuing support of workers and increased support from countries beyond Europe. Thomas knew that organized workers were still widely seen as a threat to political stability by politicians, who had fresh in their minds the Bolshevik revolution and its promotion of proletarian power. With the support of the reformed International Trade Union Federation, representing some 27 million workers and dominating labor representation on the ILO Governing Body, Thomas was confident of success in relation to the first condition. However, gaining the support of countries outside Europe was in many respects a more politically complex task. The Governing Body of the ILO was dominated by the European powers. As India and South Africa protested the Eurocentric makeup of the Governing Body, moving a resolution to include more countries from outside of Europe, it was clear to both Thomas and his deputy, Butler, that the world was changing and the ILO had to change with it. The post-war European economies were being increasingly challenged by the industrial growth of the United States and Japan, two economies whose burgeoning presence in international affairs seemed to symbolize the decline of the European powers. To survive, the ILO had to distance itself from this decline and demonstrate the global relevance of its activities.

The ILO in the inter-war period

In 1932, the executive leadership of the ILO changed following the sudden death of Albert Thomas. His successor, Harold Butler, was already sensitive to the new currents that were shaping the world.[3] While entry of the United States into the ILO remained the key objective of Butler's tenure, he remained committed to ensuring that the ILO remained relevant to smaller nations beyond Europe.

The World Economic Conference, convened in 1933 to discuss the global depression and reach some international agreement on how to revive the ailing world economy, was a failure. Proposals for the restoration of a stable international monetary standard were rejected by the United States. Thus, with little prospect of stable exchange rate arrangements, other questions requiring international agreement could not be addressed. For many, the conference seemed to demonstrate that attempts to solve the economic crisis through international co-operation were condemned to failure. The world political situation was also deteriorating. In March 1933, the National Socialist Party led by the new German chancellor, Adolf Hitler, won the German elections, having mobilized popular resentment against the peace treaty and, by June, Germany had stopped paying her foreign debts. In Italy, the National Fascist Party under Benito Mussolini began giving greater prominence to arms expenditure and military conquest. Meanwhile, in the Pacific, Japanese expansionism led to war with China in Manchuria.

The failure of the League of Nations to broker any solutions in the deteriorating global situation rendered it increasingly impotent, and morbid disillusionment began to color its activities. However, while the Great Depression and the reaction of the international community to it had a negative, and ultimately terminal, effect on the League of Nations, it had the opposite effect on the ILO. The autonomy and freedom of action which the ILO developed within the League system protected it from the political decline of its parent organization. During the Depression and in light of the League's decision to impose a general policy of austerity, relations between the two organizations became particularly tense. The determination of Albert Thomas to develop independent and direct channels of communication with government, employer and trade union representatives in member countries led to the political and functional autonomy of the ILO becoming "de facto an inviolable principle."[4] Moreover, as the League declined, the political importance of the ILO increased as the United States, and soon afterwards the Soviet Union, became members in 1934.

Concerns over the linkage between the League and the ILO had been a major factor in the United States' reluctance to become a member of the ILO.[5] As a result, between 1919 and 1934, US policy towards the ILO remained subordinated to broader US policy on the League of Nations. Two factors played an influential part in changing this position; the election of Franklin D. Roosevelt to the US presidency in 1932, and the impact of the Depression on the US economy. The fact that the United States was no more immune to the effects of the Depression than other countries came as a shock to a nation which had grown prosperous and inward-looking. A few years earlier, and on the eve of the Great Crash of 1929, President Coolidge told the legislators and people of the United States that they could "regard the present with satisfaction and anticipate the future with optimism."[6] By 1933, GNP in the United States was almost one-third less than in 1929, its credit and banking system required emergency legislation to prevent its collapse, and one in every four of its labor force was out of work. It was also the year the United States sent its first delegation to the International Labour Conference.[7]

The dramatic downturn in domestic economic activity and its impact upon jobs prompted the Roosevelt administration to examine seriously the question of ILO membership. Important in this decision was the impact of competition on the increasingly precarious US trade position. The championing of the ILO was led by Secretary of Labor Francis Perkins,[8] and stemmed from a fear that a rise in US labor standards would result in a proportional rise in its labor costs and result in a "competitive trade disadvantage and an intensification of an already disastrous unemployment problem."[9] Perkins recognized that the years of self-imposed isolationism had left the United States lacking in information on the legislative activities of other economies struggling with the Depression, and that the ILO was a primary source of that information.

For Butler, entry of the United States into the ILO had become a matter of some urgency. The contraction of domestic economic activity not only had a fundamental impact upon the world economy but also on the convention-setting activities of the ILO. Ratifications, which had peaked at 79 in 1928–29, began a downward spiral to 28 by the end of 1933.[10] For an organization whose raison d'être at that point was the setting of international labor standards, the decline was a cause for real concern. The Depression was an obvious factor in this decline. Another was the increasing reluctance of member states to ratify new conventions due to the non-participation of important competitors such as the United States and the Soviet Union.

A shift in the center of gravity: the importance of US membership and involvement

Butler believed that unemployment was the worst of all social evils. He consistently emphasized in his annual reports to the International Labour Conference that economic and financial policy was inseparable from social policy. Any search for a solution to mass unemployment and social injustice could not be conducted in isolation from other policies. It was as essential to examine the social implications of financial and economic policy as it was to consider the financial and economic implications of social policy.

Butler's vision of the general political scene was acute, as was his ability to see the dangers and opportunities that it presented.[11] This was reflected in Butler's desire to demonstrate to the United States that the ILO was a "completely independent body that formulated its own policies and administered its affairs without League interference or control."[12] Butler was also becoming increasingly frustrated at the dominance of European countries in the activities of the ILO and the League of Nations.[13] In particular, he was aware that the United States would be reluctant to take the ILO seriously until a more representative group of countries were on its Governing Body.[14] At a time when the standard-setting activities of the ILO were falling and countries were calling into question the organization's relevance, fostering the interests of non-European states became critical.

To shift its center of gravity away from Europe and to construct a more representative Governing Body was vital for the ILO's long-term survival. The Depression seemed only to underline the decay of the European powers and with it the necessity to change the focus of the ILO. It had also brought a marked increase in anti-imperialist activity, prompted by the collapse in commodity prices on which the colonial economies depended and the beginning of indigenous political and social discontent directed against European states which could no longer sustain empires "imbued with an infinite complexity of producer interests."[15] This discontent was fed by the rise of alternatives to the political and economic orthodoxies of the imperialist powers. At a time when the USSR appeared immune to the Depression and kept its workers free from the unemployment lines which grew in its wake, communism offered one alternative. Another was fascism. Its German version (National Socialism) drew from an intellectual tradition in Germany hostile to the orthodoxy of economic liberalism, and offered an apparatus of government ruthlessly determined to eradicate unemployment at all costs.

Both models (communism and fascism) appeared to respond to the Depression successfully, underlining their appeal as alternatives to the failed traditional liberal capitalist policies of the European powers. They also added further to the corrosion already spreading through the foundations of the political institutions and intellectual values of nineteenth-century liberal bourgeois society.[16] The implications of this corrosion for peace, social stability and the ILO were not lost on Butler.

We noted above that, as the Depression deepened, the standard-setting activities of the ILO slowed. In response it began to look for ways to increase those activities by increasing the relevance of the ILO and its activities, and, in particular, by addressing the impacts of the Depression. For Butler, the world beyond Europe was growing in importance economically and politically. In order to survive, he believed the ILO had to reflect this change and build an organization that had universal relevance. A significant factor in this respect was the growing power of the United States. Butler was convinced that once the United States became an ILO member, European dominance would be broken, changes in the underlying structure of power would become more visible, and broader, more inclusive international coalitions would gradually emerge. As a result, he worked hard to make US membership a reality. The United States viewed the ILO with some suspicion yet its membership remained vital to ILO survival. The issue of state sovereignty rendered ILO membership and the ratification of international labor standards a politically sensitive process. In the years between 1919 and 1934, the United States represented the most important example of these sensitivities.

Political change was the catalyst for more positive, more proactive, relations with the ILO. Following the election of the Roosevelt administration, entry of the United States in 1934 symbolized the end of European dominance and saw the ILO move into a broader, more inclusive phase in its development.

The election of the American, John G. Winant, to succeed Butler came to symbolize this change. Winant had been appointed assistant director to Butler soon after the United States joined the ILO. His presence persuaded the ILO Governing Body of Roosevelt's commitment and, in sharp contrast to the indifference and hostility shown by the United States toward the League of Nations, it demonstrated to domestic interests in the United States the importance the Roosevelt administration attached to the work of the ILO at a time when isolationist sentiment was still strong. Despite these intentions, Winant's tenure as director-general was brief, lasting only two years from 1939 to 1941. His most significant contribution during this time was to move the ILO headquarters from Geneva to Montreal for the duration of the war. Away from European hostilities, the ILO was able to continue its activities, most prominently in its technical assistance programs in Latin America. Despite the difficulties posed by the war and relocation, and with support of the United States which was keen to keep alive what was left of the international system, the ILO continued to convene its international labor conferences.

Officially, the ILO constitution required that an international labor conference be held once a year, that a governing body be elected and that a budget be approved. However, the primary reason for the decision to convene a conference was survival. Edward Phelan, who took over as acting director from Winant in 1941 and remained the ILO's executive head until after the war, argued that without a conference, the ILO ran the risk of a rapid demise. Increasingly aware that a policy of isolationism would do little for its economy after the war, and eager to prepare its electorate for the lead it wished to take in post-war reconstruction, the United States offered first New York, and then Philadelphia as conference venues.

The 1941 New York conference laid bare Phelan's desire for the ILO to be the main forum for social questions associated with post-war reconstruction and to be represented at any future peace conference. The functional logic of placing the ILO on an equal footing with all other institutions dealing with post-war reconstruction seemed clear. The ILO's knowledge and expertise in social issues were unrivalled and its argument that at the root of economic problems lay the solution to social problems was widely accepted.

The ILO's future depended upon the support of the United States. The uncertainty of its role in a post-war world in which the USA would be dominant and in which a new international system would emerge to reflect this, questioned the ILO's relevance. For Phelan, who had been one of the architects of the ILO and had worked closely with all the previous directors-general, the ILO needed to demonstrate its own dynamism and mark a prominent place for itself among the number of international institutions that would grow as post-war planning developed. In doing so, Phelan wanted to send two clear signals to ILO members; that the ILO still retained enough institutional dynamism to plan its future work despite the war and the limitations of its Montreal existence, and that the ILO intended to remain the primary organization from which any post-war regime for international labor standards would evolve.

It was against this background that Phelan called for a new conference. Its purpose was to establish the ILO's credentials as a legitimate and vital part of reconstruction plans and affirm political support for this role. The agenda comprised the ILO's reconstruction policy, proposals to integrate ILO activities with existing and future organizations for post-war reconstruction, and, in order to undertake these new functions, proposals for changes to ILO structures and constitution. The conference was held in Philadelphia from 20 April to 12 May 1944.

The outcome was the Declaration of Philadelphia. It proclaimed that labor is not a commodity, that freedom of expression and of association are essential to sustained progress, that poverty anywhere constitutes a danger to prosperity everywhere, and that the war against want should be based on concerted and continuous international effort. Critically, it placed human rights at the center of the ILO's functions for the first time. The declaration was incorporated into the ILO's constitution. As a result, it became not only a statement of the aims and purposes of the ILO in preparation for the post-war world, but also part of the constitutional obligations of ILO membership.

The inclusion of human rights at the center of the Philadelphia Declaration was significant. It was not only a key element of Phelan's re-launch of the ILO and the reformulation of its constitution as it pushed for a place at the table of post-war planning, but also argued that labor standards were an indelible part of political democracy, bound up with a growing post-war emphasis on human rights and the pursuit of industrial prosperity.[17]

The executive of the ILO now looked to the United States for leadership. As US isolationism gave way to a more international outlook, an outlook concerned that the United States' basic ideals of political pluralism and liberal democracy were under threat in Europe and Latin America, the ILO took on political significance. Moreover, significant and far reaching support was forthcoming during June 1945 when an amendment to the Dumbarton Oaks proposals setting up the United Nations Charter incorporated the ILO into the UN system.

In a number of respects the same issues which influenced support for the ILO at the end of the First World War, were evident at the end of the Second World War. The fear of communism and the post-war demands of labor nationally and internationally once again loomed large in the minds of those planning for the post-war world. More significant in

1945 was the concern that communism had spread globally to emerge as a powerful alternative to the liberal democratic system led by the United States. As a result, intergovernmental organizations such as the ILO were to become forums for tensions between the two systems.

The ILO in the post-war period

Major expansion of ILO membership followed the end of the Second World War. The Declaration of Philadelphia in 1944 had served to re-establish the basic principles of the ILO and reinvigorate its membership around a prominent role for the ILO in the post-war world. Economic planning emphasized the pursuit of open markets nurtured by an international trade system based upon rules and regulations. The post-war environment was facilitated by new international organizations through which financial assistance would be channeled. Such grand schemes, however, were not without problems. In the case of the ILO, the USSR viewed the ILO with considerable skepticism and proposed the newly established World Federation of Trade Unions (WFTU) as an alternative forum. Developing countries seeking freedom from colonial dependency remained suspicious of the ILO's Eurocentrism. Despite these concerns, and with US support, the ILO became the first specialist organization of the new United Nations organization to emerge from the wreckage of the League of Nations.

In 1948, David Morse became the second American to head the ILO. Like John G. Winant, Morse weighed up the attractions of Geneva against other opportunities he was considering, such as running for the US Senate or returning to law practice. At the time, Morse was under-secretary of labor to President Truman and the sudden death of the incumbent secretary of labor made him the natural candidate for the top job. However, it was Truman himself who asked Morse to stand for the position of director-general of the ILO and, with the active support of the British, who withdrew their own candidate, Morse was elected.

Planning to stay a couple of years "to satisfy the President and see what it was like," he was to become the longest serving head of the ILO, in position for a total of 22 years. During his tenure, Morse oversaw significant change in the ILO's structure and activities. His most immediate and in many ways most significant contribution was the expansion of the ILO's technical assistance program. There was growing recognition inside the ILO that its traditional standard-setting activities could only be sustained by training those charged with implementing the standards. Technical assistance became particularly important in those newly independent developing countries, which expanded the ILO's membership during the 1950s and 1960s. In line with the pre-war emphasis on relevance, Morse set up a network of regional and field offices to address more readily the needs of the ILO membership and permit the expansion of the technical assistance program.

With this expansion in membership came institutional growth. The International Institute for Labour Studies (IILS) was set up in 1960 as an advanced center for the study of labor and social development, with Robert Cox as one of its first directors. In 1964, the International Training Centre was established in Turin as the ILO sought to meet the vocational needs of developing countries. Both became permanent and successful institutions and reflected, first, Morse's post-war emphasis on technical co-operation and, second, a desire to demonstrate the ILO's relevance to the expanding developing country membership.

A challenging geo-political dimension to the ILO's activities also began to appear. In 1954, the USSR rejoined the organization and set about criticizing what it saw as the excessive influence of the United States in the ILO's decision-making machinery. As the USSR vied for influence in the Third World, it was highly suspicious of the expansion of US-funded technical assistance programs in developing countries. As a result, the ILO found itself embroiled in the rhetoric and tensions of the Cold War, which introduced considerable strain into its functioning and its leadership. Despite these tensions, and to the delight of Morse, who saw it as a vindication of his efforts to expand the role and influence of the ILO, in 1969 the ILO was awarded the Nobel Peace Prize for its contribution to peace through social justice.

In February 1970, and less than a year after the Nobel honor, Morse resigned. For some he had "reached the limit of his ability to avoid a crisis,"[18] his political skills exhausted trying to maintain balance between the competing interests of the superpowers. His successor, the legal expert Wilfred Jenks, fared no better, despite his pedigree. Liverpool-born Jenks joined the ILO in 1931 and worked closely with Winant and Phelan, advising the former on the ILO's move to Montreal and working with the latter in drafting the Declaration of Philadelphia.

Jenks' difficulties lay in the same tensions that exhausted Morse. The post-war growth in the welfare state had ensured support for international labor standards, as had the development of a human rights discourse that informed the adoption of key conventions on freedom of association and the right to collective bargaining. Jenks was a firm advocate of human rights and his legal expertise was regularly employed in drafting many of the ILO's initiatives in this area. However, he did not possess the political skills of Morse and, despite his deep knowledge of the ILO and the machinery which facilitated its tripartite decision making, he struggled with the many Cold War divisions which now defined ILO activities.

The 1970s proved to be something of a watershed for the ILO. Jenks' decision to appoint an assistant director from the Soviet Union was seen as an act of betrayal by a United States whose support for Jenks' nomination as director-general had been decisive and who had made it clear that they were against the Soviet appointment. A tense period followed. The pressure rose when the United States decided to cease paying its contributions to the ILO for a time.[19] The decision to begin a decade of disengagement from the ILO derived from a recurring debate over the independence of representatives from communist countries, and a broader US concern over what it perceived as the increasing politicization of motions and resolutions which had little to do with the ILO's mission. The strain on Jenks told. After only three years in office and, like Albert Thomas before him, he died while on ILO business in October 1973.

Relations between the ILO and the United States remained strained but the broader global landscape was also changing. The OPEC oil crisis erupted a few days after Jenks' untimely death, while two years earlier, and following the USA's withdrawal from the Gold Standard, the Bretton Woods Accord had disintegrated. Despite a period of rapid growth between 1972 and 1973, the sharp rise in the price of oil resulted in an inevitable fall in profitability and with it a squeeze on labor costs. Rises in inflation and unemployment questioned the sustainability of the post-war consensus on growth and social policy.

The post-war emphasis on trade unionism, collective bargaining and industrial co-operation had nurtured a corporatist ideology that resonated with the national bodies who filled the conferences and committees that were the lifeblood of ILO decision making. This emphasis took little account of the vast majority of workers in developing countries scratching out a living in the informal sector and out of the reach of the protective machinery promoted by the ILO. New developmentalist initiatives such as the UN-backed New International Economic Order highlighted the needs of the developing world and their importance to the sustainability and evolution of global trade. In this context, questions about the extent to which the ILO was serving the needs of workers in developing countries highlighted the difficulties which arose for the ILO's tripartism and decision making as it struggled to reflect the interests of the non-industrialized world.

Jenks successor, his deputy-director, Francis Blanchard, had overseen the expansion in the ILO's programs for developing countries and the decentralization of its activities. Like Morse, Blanchard's diplomatic skills were highly regarded and were subsequently employed to the full when the fragile relationship with the United States finally broke down and it withdrew from the ILO in 1977. The financial consequences were significant, with a quarter of the budget lost. Many at the time predicted the ILO's demise, while the emerging and politically influential discourse around "market distortions" and "welfare dependency" further eroded the post-war consensus in which the ILO was firmly anchored. Blanchard's response underlined the commitment to human rights and technical assistance offered to developing countries. The approach followed the ILO's successful World Employment Conference in 1976 which placed development and poverty reduction on the ILO's agenda and prepared the way for later dialogue with the World Bank and the IMF.

Despite predictions, the ILO survived its political and budgetary crisis and the United States returned to its fold in 1980. By that time, a new administration under Ronald Reagan had taken office and with it came the pre-eminence of the supply-side in formulating economic policy. In the United Kingdom, the election of the Thatcher government in 1979 heralded the dismantling of the welfare state, the erosion of labor rights, and an economic restructuring which saw significant unemployment established within the traditional heartlands of post-war trade unionism. Both administrations came to support and admire each other's approach to economic management. While domestic reform followed the Hayekian path of market liberalism, its international derivative was established in the lending policies and structural adjustment programs of the World Bank and the IMF.

Rather than watch from the sideline, and on the sideline the ILO now stood, Blanchard actively encouraged engagement with the Bretton Woods institutions. As "structural adjustment" became established in the international lexicon, in 1987 Blanchard convened a high-level meeting on Employment and Structural Adjustment involving the World Bank and IMF. The meeting called for a greater understanding and acceptance of the ILO's social and labor agenda in World Bank and IMF thinking and paved the way for closer co-operation between the three institutions.[20]

This desire for closer co-operation was initially treated with arms-length indifference by the Bretton Woods institutions. However, Blanchard's successors Michel Hansenne and Juan Somavia continued to push for closer engagement, the key to which lay in the widespread criticism and popular protests the IMF and World Bank were beginning to attract. In the context of acrimonious debates around trade and labor standards and new initiatives by the ILO such as core labor standards and Decent Work, the concept of a social dimension to globalization gained prominence.[21]

The recent period

The 1980s saw the new orthodoxy of market capitalism become the rationale for changes in employment structures and in societal attitudes toward welfarism. The post-war consensus on growth and social policy was dismantled as individualism was nurtured and individual choice became a pre-eminent concern in economic policy. In many eyes, in particularly those of its erstwhile supporters, the ILO's historical emphasis on trade unions, collective bargaining and freedom of association had become irrelevant and anachronistic. Yet the ILO survived not just by the efforts and political acumen of Blanchard and his predecessors but also by virtue of the mounting social costs generated by the new orthodoxy.

With the collapse of Soviet socialism in Eastern and Central Europe, the blueprint of structural adjustment was spread out across the economic landscape of the post-communist economies. The social costs of this adjustment began to attract criticism. Globalization, social justice, and poverty reduction, became more prominent in popular discourse as social divisions increased. Labor protection became a casualty of market deregulation as the floor on the price of labor was reduced both as a bargained wage settlement, and as a legislative cost associated with, for example, health and safety and minimum wage requirements.

While the ILO struggled for relevance in the national context, the debates surrounding the conclusion of the GATT Uruguay Round offered a different story. The post-war pursuit of an open trade system under the GATT paved the way for new competitors to enter the international marketplace. The goods of export-oriented economies, particularly those of Southeast Asia, became more prominent in the shopping centers of the United States and Europe and called into question the international competitiveness of Western firms. Complaints were lodged with governments over what were perceived as the uncompetitive practices of some countries in their utilization of cheap labor. Where was the ILO to ensure that such countries abided by international labor standards? Was not labor exploitation a moral rather than a protectionist issue? Should not governments be ensuring that international trade be fair and not an excuse for ignoring social justice?

Such calls became more and more prominent as concerns over globalization grew and international business in developed economies pressured their governments to address "unfair trade practices." The tensions thrust the ILO back into the political limelight and to the forefront of debate over trade, labor standards and a social dimension to globalization.

Conclusion

By dint of strategic positioning, artfully conceived by successive directors-general, the ILO survived the demise of the League of Nations, forged a role in the post-Second World War world order, and co-existed with a Washington Consensus opposed to many of the principles upon which the ILO was founded. However, when Blanchard handed over the reins to Michel Hansenne in 1989, much remained to be done to consolidate the status and purpose of the ILO in the modern international order. Blanchard recognized the work that needed to be done in his own overtures to the Bretton Woods institutions. His successors would be required to drive changes in the strategic positioning and operational set-up of the ILO to support that consolidation. Chapters 3 to 7 explain and assess their success in meeting that challenge, but, first, in Chapter 2, we provide a brief outline of the operational aspects of the ILO.

2 Structure and organization of the ILO

In the previous chapter, we illustrated how the expansion of the ILO beyond Europe was rooted in the vision of Albert Thomas and subsequent directors-general, and a need for the ILO to be seen as an institution of global, and not simply, European relevance. The current ILO tradition emphasizes standard setting and human rights in an organizational structure that seeks to demonstrate its relevance in many ways. In particular, it does so by the establishment of offices and delivery of programs in member states and in regions around the world. In this chapter, we examine the structures and processes that govern ILO activity and facilitate the often complex relationship between its tripartite partners and that broader global reach.

ILO structure and governance[1]

Like most organizations, the structures and processes that constitute ILO activities have evolved over the years. Important in this organizational development have been the needs and aspirations of member states, particularly with regard to the training and development of executive officers responsible for ILO activity. Equally important in the governance of the ILO has been the desire by successive directors-general to maintain a global presence beyond the Geneva headquarters. The global structure of the ILO with, for example, regional offices in South America and Asia, has been instrumental in maintaining dialogue with social partners on issues of regional concern. In the same vein, the International Institute for Labour Studies has helped to provide important research to inform social policy discussions. The ILO has acted as a global forum for debate, developing and commissioning major research that contributes to policy formulation, and providing education programs for workers, employers and labor administrators. A sophisticated contribution to this didactic capacity is the Turin-based

International Training Centre (ITC). The ITC has provided education and training for those charged with implementing ILO agreements at the national level since 1965, and is extending its outreach through greater utilization of new technologies in web-based distance learning.

The International Labour Office

Originally housed on the shore of Lake Geneva in a building now occupied by the World Trade Organization, the ILO's administrative headquarters, the International Labour Office, sits amidst a constellation of international organizations located in Geneva, including the United Nations, the World Health Organization and the International Red Cross. Home to the permanent secretariat and location for many conferences, workshops, briefings and the like, the International Labour Office is the ILO's operational headquarters, research center and publishing house. It is a large and imposing building that stands in extensive grounds, with a considerable store of both external and internal works of art, and in many ways is symbolic of the large administrative structure that is necessary to run a 182-member-country organization.

Underpinning ILO organizational activity are the strategic objectives proposed by directors-general and agreed by the ILO Governing Body. Currently, these are to:

- promote and realize standards and fundamental principles and rights at work;
- create greater opportunities for women and men to secure decent employment and income;
- enhance the coverage and effectiveness of social protection for all; and
- strengthen tripartism and social dialogue.

In total, the ILO employs some 2,500 staff worldwide overseen by its Geneva-based executive (see Figure 2.1).

It operated in the 2008/2009 year with an income of US$565 million.

Tripartism

The ILO has a tripartite structure of governance and decision making that remains unique within the UN. It is premised on the belief that dialogue between workers and employers has a fundamental role to play in the development of society. The ILO offers an institutional structure in which this dialogue is focused on the common good through a system of tripartite organization and decision making. Each year, ILO

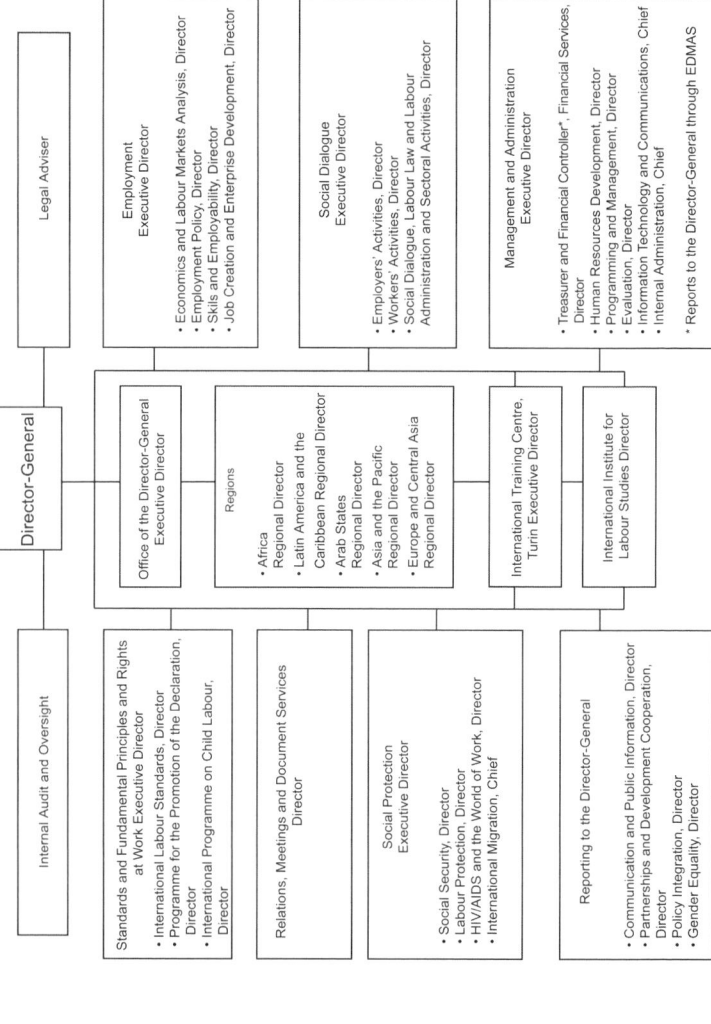

Figure 2.1 International Labour Office senior management structure

member states are invited to send representatives of the "social partners" (two government, one employer and one labor representative) to the annual International Labour Conference. Each has the right to speak and vote independently. The ILO Governing Body also reflects this tripartite structure, comprising 28 government members, 14 employer and 14 worker members. Ten of the government seats are permanently held by "States of Chief Industrial Importance" (Brazil, China, France, Germany, India, Italy, Japan, the Russian Federation, the United Kingdom, and the United States). The other government members are elected by the Conference every three years, while labor and employer representatives are elected via a separate electoral process. Working within and around this structure are various tripartite and expert committees that focus on particular industries or key issues. In the recent past, issues that have occupied the energies of ILO members include a proposed link between trade and labor standards; the use and exploitation of child labor (which has impelled the introduction of new labor standards); and the establishment of country-level initiatives such as the International Program on the Elimination of Child Labor (IPEC) which promotes alternatives to child labor through over 1,000 ILO-sponsored initiatives worldwide.

This tripartite activity is extended to include the promotion in member states of national-level "social dialogue" between labor and employer organizations, covering a broad spectrum of social and economic issues and supported by an extensive network of technical co-operation. This process is usually managed from permanent offices established in five regions from which ILO field programs are co-ordinated. From this regional platform, the ILO is able to engage more readily with national-level social partners and organize conferences, seminars and similar events on regional issues. This structure reflects a desire, established in the early years of the ILO's institutional life, to maintain a visible and active relevance beyond its Geneva headquarters. In addition, the ILO maintains 40 field offices around the world which, among other activities, facilitate visits of over 600 technical experts engaged in ILO-related missions each year.

International labor standards

The ILO is most commonly associated with the promulgation of international labor standards. One of its principal achievements has been to expand labor protection into the domain of human rights and tie these to the pursuit of freedom and economic progress. At root is an acknowledgement that social problems are political as well as economic in nature and that economic security and equality of opportunity are basic human rights. International standards are set on a wide range of labor-related issues. Key outcomes from the International Labour Conference include legislative instruments which, once adopted by ILO member states, constitute what is broadly termed the International Labour Code.

The International Labour Code comprises two related elements. *Conventions* are agreed at the annual International Labour Conference and become legally binding instruments through their adoption into national legislative frameworks. *Recommendations* provide member states with guidance on legislative development, labor policy and management practice. For example, the activities of the International Program on the Elimination of Child Labor (IPEC) referred to earlier are underpinned by two key conventions, the Minimum Age Convention 1973 (no. 138) and the Worst Forms of Child Labour Convention 1999 (no. 182). Both are supplemented by related recommendations. In this example, these legislative provisions form part of an integrated program of social protection that focuses international agreements, national action, technical co-operation, and a system of supervision on IPEC priority target groups such as bonded child laborers, children working in hazardous occupations and young working children (those below 12 years of age).

Conventions and recommendations emerge over time. In general terms, an issue will arise in ILO discussions, brought up by one or more of the social partners. Discussion will ensue within and between the social partners, supported by research and analysis provided by ILO specialists. As the issue becomes clearer, a draft convention or recommendation may emerge, and will then be subjected to further analysis and amendment. When the groundwork is complete, the proposed new convention or recommendation may be introduced at the annual International Labour Conference, for discussion and possible endorsement. Once agreed by all parties, member states are encouraged to ratify the new measure, that is, incorporate its provisions into domestic legislative provision.

As we discuss later in the book, the calls for a Social Clause that dogged the fledgling WTO in 1995, and made frequent appearances in WTO ministerials thereafter, made reference to prioritized ILO conventions identified as "core" labor standards. Until the 1998 Declaration on Fundamental Principals and Rights at Work, agreement on core standards was confined to those dealing with freedom of association, specifically Freedom of Association and Protection of the Right to Organise (Convention 87) and the Right to Organise and Collective Bargaining (Convention 98). This is because support for the principle of freedom of association was enshrined both in the preamble to the ILO constitution and in the Declaration of Philadelphia 1944, and thus constituted a principle binding upon all member states of the ILO. However, the 1998 declaration specified four fundamental principles and rights at work underpinned by eight core conventions (see Box 2.1).

Approximately half of the OECD countries have ratified most or all of the core conventions while, at the other end of the scale, the United States, a prime supporter of the Social Clause idea, has ratified only two of them (Convention 105 on the Abolition of Forced Labour, and

---

Box 2.1 Eight fundamental or "core" conventions contained in the Declaration on Fundamental Principles and Rights at Work, 1998

Fundamental ILO conventions

Eight ILO conventions have been identified by the ILO's Governing Body as being fundamental to the rights of human beings at work, irrespective of levels of development of individual member states. These rights are a precondition for all the others in that they provide for the necessary implements to strive freely for the improvement of individual and collective conditions of work.

Freedom of association and the right to collective bargaining

C87

Freedom of Association and Protection of the Right to Organise Convention, 1948

Establishes the right of all workers and employers to form and join a union of their own choosing.

C98

Right to Organise and Collective Bargaining Convention, 1949

Protects against anti-union discrimination, acts of interference and promotes collective bargaining.

Abolition of forced or compulsory labor

C29

Forced Labour Convention, 1930

With certain exceptions such as military service, convict labor and emergencies, requires the suppression of all forms of forced labor.

C105

Abolition of Forced Labour Convention, 1957

Prohibits the use of any form of forced or compulsory labor for particular means, such as political coercion, taking part in strike activity, the expression of political views, etc.

Elimination of discrimination in employment

C100

Equal Remuneration Convention, 1951

Calls for equal pay and benefits between men and women for work of equal value.

C111

Discrimination (Employment and Occupation) Convention, 1958

Calls for the prohibition of all forms of discrimination in employment, training and working conditions.

Convention 182 on the Abolition of the Worst Forms of Child Labour). In fact, the United States has ratified only 14 of the ILO's 188 conventions. The United States Department of Labor explains that the low rate of ratification follows from:

> three ground rules ensuring that no ILO convention will be ratified unless or until US law and practice, at both the federal and state

levels, is in full conformity with its provisions. By necessity, the legal review process prior to ratification is complex and lengthy. Even in the absence of formal ratification, the United States has demonstrated on many occasions that its laws and practices meet or exceed virtually every ILO convention and that the law is backed up by enforcement mechanisms.[2]

The low rate of ratification also reflects the political realities surrounding the United States' involvement in the ILO, and domestic political debate around internationally imposed labor standards.

Supervisory mechanisms

Over the years, the ILO has developed a number of mechanisms for supervising the implementation of conventions and recommendations and maintaining general adherence to its International Labour Code. There are two forms of supervisory mechanism in operation at the ILO, the regular system and one requiring special procedures. The regular system involves the examination of reports submitted by member states detailing the action they have taken to implement ratified conventions. Such reports are first examined by the Committee of Experts on the Application of Conventions and Recommendations, which is appointed by the Governing Body to make comments or direct requests on states' adherence to conventions that they have ratified. Observations are made in cases where there has been serious or persistent failure to abide by the obligations under the ratified convention(s). Serious contraventions identified by the Committee of Experts are passed on to, and examined by, the International Labour Conference's Tripartite Committee on the Application of Conventions and Recommendations. This may consider individual cases that have been identified by the Committee of Experts to warrant particular attention. In such cases, the government in question is invited to make written and oral statements to the committee, which then issues a report on their findings. This report is then discussed at a plenary session of the Conference and, if adopted, is published and sent to the government concerned.

The special procedures process is somewhat more complex, involving three distinct processes. These are:

- Procedure for representation on the application of ratified conventions—under this procedure, any employer or worker organization at either national or international level can make a complaint to the ILO if it deems that a member state has failed to meet the obligations of a convention that it (the state) has ratified. On issues related to trade union rights, the matter may be referred to the Committee on Freedom of Association (see below) or an ad hoc tripartite committee, which meets in private and can request further information, including an appearance before the committee, to determine the validity and seriousness of the complaint. Its conclusions and recommendations are then submitted to the ILO Governing Body for a decision.

- Procedure for complaints on the application of ratified conventions—under this procedure, the onus is on a member state to submit a complaint against another member state, which it believes has not implemented a convention that it has ratified. Here the Governing Body may initiate a Commission of Inquiry to investigate the complaint and, if necessary, submit a report containing recommendations. The government concerned is expected to meet these recommendations within a specified timescale. There is then a three month hiatus during which the government can either accept or reject the recommendations of the commission. If accepted, the Committee of Experts is then charged to monitor the implementation of the recommendations. If they are rejected, the case can be referred to the International Court of Justice, the decision of which is final.
- Special procedure for complaints regarding freedom of association—the main characteristic of this procedure is that complaints can be made against a member state by any of the social partners if it is believed that the state is in contravention of freedom of association protections, irrespective of whether the relevant conventions have been ratified or not. This is possible as all members of the ILO are bound by its constitution, which, among other things, upholds the principle of freedom of association and requires all members to abide by this principle whether or not they have ratified the relevant conventions. Two special bodies come into play under this procedure, the Committee on Freedom of Association and the Fact-Finding and Conciliation Commission on Freedom of Association, both of which are convened by the Governing Body. The role of the former is to protect freedom of association for workers and employers. It meets three times a year under an independent chair appointed from outside the Governing Body. A key feature of the committee is its ability to undertake in-country investigations (albeit subject to the consent of the country concerned) and, in a "name and shame" approach, make very public the complaint and subsequent reports in cases in which the government concerned has obstructed the investigation. In the case of the commission, it can also investigate

alleged violations of freedom of association but include in its remit complaints against governments which are not part of the ILO but members of the United Nations. In these instances, the case is referred to the commission by the United Nations Economic and Social Council (ECOSOC). In general, the commission follows the same procedure as a Commission of Inquiry (see above) but in attempting to resolve complaints before it, conciliation can play a part in its deliberations.

Technical co-operation and capacity building

Originally set up in the early 1950s to support developing nations, technical co-operation programs now account for over half of the ILO budget and cover activities in some 140 countries and territories, from training entrepreneurs in small business administration to assisting governments in revising labor legislation. The emphasis on linking international agreements with national activity reflects a long-held ILO emphasis on "demonstrable relevance." This seeks to ensure that, in pursuit of its mandate, the ILO has a visible and active presence within those member states in most need of its support and expertise. Increasingly, ILO technical co-operation is run in conjunction with poverty reduction programs operated by the United Nations, the World Bank and the International Monetary Fund (IMF), underlining the ILO commitment to ensuring that social protection issues form part of an integrated framework of economic and financial aid.

The contemporary overriding purpose of the ILO's technical co-operation activities is the pursuit of the Decent Work agenda (see Chapter 6). This is a push to make international agreements in which the ILO's principles and involvement are more visible and more relevant to national development needs. To this end, the ILO relies upon its network of regional, area and branch offices established in over 40 countries and charged with developing dialogue with its tripartite constituents at the local level. A greater emphasis on capacity building and co-ordinated work with multilateral organizations such as the World Bank and national governmental agencies such as the United Kingdom's Department for International Development (DFID) has facilitated the operation of over 1,000 technical co-operation programs globally.

Increasingly, ILO technical co-operation is run in conjunction with poverty reduction programs operated by the UN, the World Bank and the IMF, underlining ILO commitment to ensuring that social protection issues form part of an integrated framework of economic and financial aid. The activities of the ILO in this area have developed from a strategic move to become more engaged with the Bretton Woods institutions in a social policy oriented system of global governance. Speeches of ILO directors-general Juan Somavia and Michel Hansenne have consistently emphasized the ILO's desire to gain a place at the "top table" of international institutions engaged in global economic governance.

Once describing the current system as an "archipelago of unconnected islands," Somavia has used the platform of his annual speech to the International Labour Conference to call for greater social coherence in the lending and poverty alleviation policies of the IMF and the World Bank. While there have been reciprocal invitations to conferences and committee meetings, progress in involving the ILO in IMF and World Bank affairs has been slow. The main area in which ILO expertise in social issues has been utilized by the IMF and World Bank has been in poverty reduction. However, as Chapter 7 indicates, the post-2007 global financial crisis provided an important opportunity for the ILO to play a role at the heart of international responses to the crisis.

The integration of the ILO's Decent Work agenda into World Bank and IMF initiatives on poverty reduction is enabled and monitored through the Poverty Reduction Strategy Papers (PRSPs). Initiated in 1999 by the Bretton Woods institutions, the PRSP process was introduced as a way of ensuring that concessional financing through the IMF's Poverty Reduction and Growth Facility (PRGF) and the World Bank group's International Development Associations (IDA) effectively addressed poverty reduction. The link with the ILO Decent Work agenda came as an outcome of growing global criticism of the IFIs' narrow focus and Somavia's own push to get ILO member states to help put social justice issues on to IFI agendas.

In a shift away from a traditional emphasis on dialogue with state ministries, an essential element of the PRSPs is their emphasis on the national ownership of programs, based upon widespread consultation with labor and civil society groups. In consequence, and in recognition of the need for greater policy coherence across multilateral institutions, synergies between the ILO's Decent Work agenda, integrating the so-called four pillars of ILO activities (employment, social protection, social dialogue and labor rights and standards) and the poverty reduction focus of the Bretton Woods institutions, were acknowledged and a platform for closer co-operation, linking poverty reduction with employment intensive economic growth, was established. This resulted in a series of pilot projects funded by the United Kingdom in which the ILO developed a systematic approach to involvement in the PRSP process, integrating a Decent Work perspective into planning, implementation, outcomes and evaluation. Following the conclusion of these pilot projects, the ILO approach is now being rolled out to some 35 countries, comprising over half the total number of countries engaged with the multilateral PRSP process. The PRSP process remains the central platform of the multilateral financial and aid architecture, guiding the national and development planning, budget allocation and development aid for over 70 countries.

Multilateral Organisation Performance Assessment Network

The ILO's attempts at national level dialogue have not always been successful. The resources placed at its disposal have struggled to match its ambition. Its technical co-operation program is smaller than that of other UN agencies, while issues of employment and decent work have not been very visible in the Millennium Development Goals (MDGs) agendas nor in the thinking of development agencies preoccupied with providing the basics of food, water, shelter and health in the war against poverty. A report on the ILO in 2006 by the Multilateral Organisation Performance Assessment Network (MOPAN),[3] a group of donor countries which monitor and assess the performance of multilateral organizations in developing countries in which MOPAN members are active, provoked much thought and internal discussion. A striking finding of the survey was how little was known about the ILO in the countries in which it was active. A strong correlation was found to exist between the strength and visibility of the ILO in a country and an understanding of what it is, what it does and what it stands for. Unsurprisingly, this correlation exists in countries in which the ILO has a permanent presence, such as a regional or country office. However, where the ILO presence is largely confined to individual projects or periodic missions, the correlation is weak. In some of these latter cases, the visibility of the ILO was so low that country reports submitted to MOPAN did not bother to mention it. The observation stimulated on-going discussions and reviews of ILO field structures, and subsequent plans to reconfigure these structures to support better the Decent Work agenda and the general recommendations for UN reform.

One outcome has been the establishment of Decent Work Country Programs (DWCP) as an organizing structure for mainstreaming the Decent Work agenda in national development activities. DWCP vary from country to country in size, composition, and particular development focus, but all offer resources and advice that pursue Decent Work objectives. Current proposals place a greater emphasis on regional linkages and the incorporation of a more robust and focused technical advice capacity. They provide for a two-tier structure that simplifies reporting lines between country offices (which may serve more than one country) and their regional counterparts. A key innovation is the introduction of Decent Work Technical Support Teams (DWTs), which will be established in each region. These will be responsible for co-ordinating activity around the ILO's four strategic objectives and support country offices in the design and implementation of DWCP. Under the proposed structure, the number of regional offices will remain the same (five), sub-regional offices will disappear (15 to 0) and the number of country offices will increase (31 to 46). The latter will be serviced by 13 newly established DWTs.

Conclusion: the continuing focus on labor protection

The complex nature of the ILO is vividly reflected in its structural organization and in its system of governance. The activities of its Geneva headquarters are complemented by a web of regional offices that provide local points of contact and on-the-ground intelligence. The introduction and protection of labor standards remain at the heart of ILO activities and provide an explicit point of reference in the political complexities associated with its unique tripartite structure. It may be that those who now direct the International Labour Office prefer to talk about social partnership rather than labor interests, the development of social protection rather than labor standards, and seek to promote and defend human rights rather than labor rights. Yet the focus is still on labor protection, be it the worst forms of child labor, the plight of migrant labor or those found marginalized to the periphery of work and society. To echo Albert Thomas, labor and the interests of labor are the raison d'être of the ILO, and continue to provide its philosophical and organizational coherence.

The ILO developed its structure and practice to support the promotion of labor protection. An effective organization was needed to support the survival strategies developed by successive directors-general, as we discussed in Chapter 1. However, as is the case for any organization, the ILO has had to adapt to meet new challenges. This is particularly true for the recent period since the 1980s, when the ILO restructured its principles and its structure to meet the challenge of globalization. In Chapter 3, we discuss the ILO's analysis of the challenges posed by globalization to the ILO's principles and practice.

3 The ILO and globalization

As we have shown in previous chapters, the ILO has survived its sometimes rocky history as a result of a combination of factors, primarily astute leadership, the ability to maintain its relevance, and the quality of its technical activities. However, when the Belgian, Michel Hansenne, became director-general in 1998, the ILO was once again in need of renovation and refocusing. The world in which the ILO operated was changing, as Hansenne's predecessor, Francis Blanchard, had recognized, and, once again, the ILO's ability to position itself as an important player in that new world was called into question.

The ILO and market fundamentalism

The overarching challenge to the ILO was globalization and the role to be played by the ILO and its international labor standards regime.[1] By the 1980s, it was clear that the assimilation of firms, national economies, and regions into an integrated international economy was increasing in pace and extent, not only as a result of the movement of foreign direct investment (FDI) and related international investment strategies, but also because of the effects of new technology, increasingly complex global financial arrangements, liberalization of trade and investment regimes, the emergence of supra-national economic blocs, internationalization of labor markets, and other related factors. Globalization commanded its own ideology, which became dominant through the 1970s and 1980s. Advocates of market fundamentalism, the policy prescriptions sometimes known as neo-liberalism or supply-side economics, extolled the virtues of much that globalization promised.

The notion of a global market, fettered only by the most necessary of regulation, captured the imagination of market fundamentalists. This notion was embedded in the "Washington Consensus," the globally dominant economic policy prescription for all economies, especially the less developed, which in part emerged from the international financial institutions (the International Monetary Fund and the World Bank), based in Washington.[2] Other processes supported the Consensus approach. The collapse of the Soviet bloc, the market-driven reforms in China and the dominance of the United States in the world order combined to support globalization. For much of the period between 1970 and 2000, any challenges to the driving logic of globalization, intellectual or policy-driven, were treated with something verging on incredulity by economic orthodoxy. Governments either supported wholeheartedly that orthodoxy or, if not wholly convinced by its arguments, were forced by internal and external pressures to accept most of its wisdom. Corporatist traditions, which many believed were conducive to ILO-type interventions, were weakened. "Modern" social democracy tended to adopt many of the economic prescriptions associated with market fundamentalism.[3]

Domestic policy was substantially revised as the new orthodoxy became established. Its preferred policy settings favored free trade and the end of protection for domestic industries, and argued for unregulated exchange rates and the liberalization of the financial sector. The unregulated international movement of capital was promoted. State sector assets were privatized where possible, or, if kept in public ownership, "corporatized" and run in a private-sector manner. In social policy, market fundamentalists favored an individualist philosophy and an end to what was described as a dependence on the state. Welfare benefits were cut, food and fuel subsidies were reduced or abolished, unemployment benefits were reduced and made more difficult to access, social housing was privatized, and charges were introduced into education.

In employment policy, labor markets were deregulated in the expectation that flexible labor markets would contribute to improved productivity and greater competitiveness. Under the banner of "freeing" the individual from the "monopoly" of trade union powers, measures were introduced to increase the power of management in employment relations, and reduce trade union influence. Trade unions found it to be increasingly difficult to maintain membership levels, and union density fell. The incidence of collective bargaining similarly fell away. From an ILO perspective, one of the social partners (trade unions) became substantially weaker. Meanwhile, the incidence of tripartism as an approach to problem-solving declined as a bipartite government-business alliance became dominant. Contemporaneously, management utilized new human resource management strategies, designed to exclude trade unions and create unitary, company-based employment relations.

The rationale for, and operations of, the ILO were at odds with the principles of market fundamentalism. From a fundamentalist perspective, tripartism, the heart of the ILO model, was not simply outdated. It was dangerous, for it proposed the distorting and inefficient managing of market relations. It gave status to trade unions, which, in the fundamentalist view, were monopoly agents manipulating the price of labor to the advantage of some (a minority), and to the disadvantage of others (the majority, including non-unionized workers and consumers). Advocates of market fundamentalism saw this as clear evidence of the out-datedness of the ILO and its thinking.

The ILO's concern for social policy was, in fundamentalist eyes, also misguided. Its consolidation in the inter-war years' economic crisis established for fundamentalists the contemporary danger associated with the ILO's "Keynesian" welfarism. There was no legitimate role for the ILO to play in this context, and so a further question mark hung over its relevance.

Underpinning this skepticism was a much deeper concern about the true intentions of global agencies such as the ILO. Advocates of market fundamentalism question the need for regulation of any sort, and have grave doubts about global regulation, that is, the international regulation of business, trade or people by international agreements. Where such regulation is clearly in tune with market fundamentalist philosophy, as, for example, in the case of the World Trade Organization, those doubts are assuaged. This was not the case for the ILO. The ILO's history, structure and emphases sat outside much fundamentalist thinking. Inevitably, business thinking, and that of politicians and government officials, became more critical of the ILO and its usefulness came into question once again. Inevitably, then, the capacity to maintain its relevance and its status became a driving concern within the ILO. This pressure was exacerbated by international funding regimes which gave the Bretton Woods institutions control over great resources, access to which was an important operational consideration for the ILO.

That concern was urgent. Standing has described much of the 1970s and 1980s as a "period of intellectual shrinkage, as it [the ILO] floundered in the face of the initial phase of the Global Transformation that has been called globalization."[4] Indeed, he argues that, after the highpoint of 1969, marked by its receipt of a Nobel Prize, the ILO's strategic, financial and political problems grew. These were caused, in part, by the retreat from the ILO by the United States in 1975,[5] and by what Standing implies were misguided priority issues—the "informal sector" and "basic needs"—and the "grandiosely-named World Employment Programme" (WEP). We will return to Standing's analysis later.

The ILO's response to this new challenge to its relevance was tried and tested. It renewed itself in terms of focus and dynamism, turning the challenge of globalization into an opportunity to reposition itself. As in the inter-war years, it did so in part by raising to the director-general's role two leaders, the Belgian, Michel Hansenne, and the Chilean, Juan Somavia, willing to tackle the challenge of repositioning the ILO. Under their leadership, a response to the challenges of globalization and market fundamentalism was implemented after 1994. That response involved, first, the development of an ILO perspective on globalization. Second, there was renewal of the ILO mandate to meet the new challenge. Third, there was a refocusing of the ILO's organization and work streams in response to that challenge, involving the extension of the ILO's traditional focus on labor standards into a broader understanding of contemporary work. The ILO's response to globalization is the focus of the remainder of this chapter.

A fair globalization?

Speaking to the 1994 International Labour Conference on the occasion of the ILO's 75th anniversary, Director-General Michel Hansenne called for the ILO to make a new assessment of its aims and goals.[6] The need for this assessment, argued Hansenne, was driven by "a drastic acceleration in the globalization of the economy." Globalization, he said, benefited some, but disadvantaged others, and challenged established thinking within and beyond the ILO. Signaling a future role for the ILO, he argued that the social dimensions of globalization had to be better understood and given more weight in the international community. He made the case that the social dimensions of globalization should be fully taken into account in the management (that is, regulation) of the global economy. Moreover, he explicitly set a course for the ILO to understand globalization and what it might mean for the ILO. In his 1994 speech, Hansenne presaged a renewal of the ILO designed to re-establish a relevance and status eroded in the previous two decades.

Hansenne was, in institutional terms, marking out the ILO's turf in the new global order, much as the Declaration of Philadelphia in 1944 had asserted the ILO's reach beyond labor market matters. However, his commentaries were far more than an institutional positioning of the ILO. Like his predecessors in the inter-war years, Hansenne believed keenly in the positive contribution to be made by the ILO to understanding, and developing, the social dimensions of globalization. Despite forceful debate in the International Labour Conference around his message, it was to be a powerful factor in future refocusing of the ILO's activities.

In subsequent years, the social dimensions of globalization became a leitmotif of ILO thinking and innovation. They rest at the heart of the 1998 Declaration of Fundamental Principles and Rights at Work and the 2008 Declaration on Social Justice for a Fair Globalisation, the debate about trade and labor standards, and they became a key element in the definition of Decent Work, which, post-1999, lay at the heart of a renewed ILO agenda.

A seminal, if controversial, ILO initiative on globalization was the World Commission on the Social Dimensions of Globalisation, established in 2001 and reporting in 2004.[7] Co-chaired by Tarja Halonen and Benjamin Mkapa, respectively presidents of Finland and Tanzania, the Commission was an "eminent persons group" asked to scope the impact of contemporary globalization and suggest ways in which its social dimensions could be furthered. Its final report, *A Fair Globalisation: Creating Opportunities for All*,[8] attempts a balanced interpretation of globalization, accepting that it is happening, that some have benefited from it, and that there are important strengths in the market economy.

Notwithstanding these positive outcomes, the Commission identified some primary concerns. For example, has globalization favored some at the expense of others, or has it increased the rate of development in poor countries and contributed to a reduction of world poverty? What have been the adjustment costs of globalization in advanced economies? Have the "tiger" economies (in Asia particularly) been able to maintain economic growth and contain the social costs of adjustment? Do we fully understand the social, rather than economic, impact of globalization? In answer to these questions, and many others, the commission concluded that there was an urgent need to build a fair and inclusive globalization. Implicit in this conclusion was the opportunity for the ILO to become a leading agency or broker in that building process. The Commission also argued that the public debate was "frozen in the ideological certainties of entrenched positions and fragmented in a variety of special interests." Again, the subtext offered a key role to the ILO in breaking this impasse.

The Commission offered a strategy for change, with two key dimensions: a range of initiatives designed to increase the fairness of global integration, and a call for effective mobilization to drive those initiatives. The initiatives confronted five pressing issues: national governance, global governance, the quality of international policies, the accountability of institutions, and mobilizing for change.

Recommendations in relation to national governance addressed, amongst others, the need for a strong democratic political system, sound institutions, a focus on sustainability and a strong civil society. They also addressed issues close to the ILO's traditional agenda and at odds with the market fundamentalist tradition; for example, an important commitment to human rights, a strong role for the state in the provision of essential services and social protection, the importance of decent work for economic success and social cohesion, and a close alignment of national policies and global interests.

Turning to global governance, the Commission argued that existing imbalances in the outcomes of globalization required major reform of international governance. Using a notion unloved by market fundamentalists (fairness), the Commission sought fairness in four areas of the global economy. On trade, the Commission argued against unfair advantage held by the advanced economies in the WTO system and demanded a fairer deal for the less-developed economies. Free trade was also rejected as a panacea; instead, it should be one facet of a balanced, sustainable global growth model, which includes employment considerations.

On global production systems, the Commission called for more consistent and coherent frameworks for FDI and cross-border competition policy. Underpinning this call was the view that the less-developed economies have been disadvantaged by current arrangements.

On the international financial system, the Commission argued for better organization, and a greater effort on the part of the system to promote sustainability and to improve the financial circumstances of poor economies. In particular, the Commission called for a greater voice for poor economies in the reform of the global financial system, greater efforts to control financial volatility and contagion, a pragmatic and cautious approach to capital account liberalization in poor economies, and further efforts to reform the debt situation afflicting the less developed economies.

On labor, the Commission emphasized the need for greater respect for core labor standards and fair regulation of cross-border movements of people. Steps to be taken included increasing the capacity of the ILO to promote core labor standards, ensuring that other international agencies also promoted these standards, and building a multilateral framework to regulate in a fair and transparent way the cross-border movement of people.

The Commission raised a wide range of recommendations in relation to what it described as international policy. Many addressed broad development issues and the need for effective global macroeconomic management. Included were calls for socially responsible investment, improved investment in education, international support for domestic social protection measures, and more social dialogue, especially on the global production system. From an ILO perspective, the call for Decent Work to be made a global goal was important.

The Commission addressed institutional accountability in terms of state and multilateral actors, on the one hand, and non-state actors, on the other. At the state and multilateral level, it called for major reform, arguing for revisions of voting rights in the Bretton Woods institutions (to favor less-developed economies), higher levels of participation in the WTO, better evaluation and monitoring of interventions by multilateral agencies, more funding to international agencies, and the creation of a Global Council on Global Governance. Again from an ILO perspective, the Commission's call for greater emphasis on and coherence in policies to improve quality of life for people, greater public accountability for international agencies, and the extension of parliamentary oversight to the multilateral system (via a Global Parliamentary Group), were important. In relation to non-state actors, the Commission offered challenging recommendations. In particular, it argued for stronger, formal engagement between the Bretton Woods institutions and labor and business. It also charged the ILO to promote corporate social responsibility (CSR) initiatives at national and international levels.

Progress, argued the Commission, rests on effective mobilization of people and institutions. Effective mobilization has three dimensions: changes within existing institutions, new institutional initiatives, and broader and deeper dialogue at national and international levels. Existing institutions should reflect on the extent to which they are involved in a broad dialogue, especially with those most affected by their interventions. They should, suggested the Commission, address their commitment in their activities to "universal values and human rights." New institutions were proposed. Policy Coherence Initiatives across international institutions should contribute to a fair and inclusive globalization. Multi-stakeholder Policy Development Dialogues across international institutions should contribute to policy development. A Globalisation Policy Forum should provide a regular platform for commentary on and assessment of the social dimensions of globalization.

The Commission's recommendations for a fairer globalization were often radical and, therefore, challenging. They described their proposals as "ambitious but feasible." Their goal was to establish a framework for a sustainable globalization, which took into account people and their rights, cultural identities and aspirations. Whilst not stated in the report, the Commission framed an alternative to the market fundamentalist approach to globalization. The alternative accepted the role of markets in general, and some tenets of the market fundamentalist approach; for example, sound macroeconomic fundamentals. However, it diverged from the market fundamentalist tradition in key ways. Its focus on fairness, domestic and global regulation, social dialogue, Decent Work, a strong state providing social protection, the role of civil society, and the reformation of many international institutions was at odds with the market fundamentalists' approach. It was, conversely, entirely consistent with ILO tradition, stretching back to ILO responses to the economic crisis of the inter-war years. The Commission's recommendations declared internationally that the ILO had a framework for managing globalization, at once different from the dominant economic orthodoxy, yet consistent with ILO traditions.

Director-General Somavia's response to the Commission's report captures that constancy.[9] A strong theme in his response was the timely challenge to the ILO posed by the Commission's report. As he put it:

> [the report] brings to our memory defining moments in the history of the ILO when our predecessors felt the need to signal a clear political direction. I believe that today we are facing a similar challenge. There are precious moments in history when opportunities come and go. Seizing them requires vision to identify the circumstances and courage to take decisions.

Somavia highlighted the foresight shown by the ILO's tripartite process in establishing the Commission and the importance of the social partners in providing responses to the challenges it posed. In doing so, he also identified the technical capacity within the ILO (its epistemic community, working alongside the social partners, that is, "the real actors") as the ILO's comparative advantage in responding to globalization. If globalization is challenging, then the ILO has the technical capacity and the traditions to meet that challenge.

Somavia also identified Decent Work[10] as a global goal, a key recommendation of the Commission, at the center of any new system of global governance. Why should Decent Work be central to global governance? The answer lies in its foundation in the core principles of the ILO which, argued Somavia, are central to sustainable global governance. These principles are, ran the argument, the guarantee of fairness and inclusion in global governance, and, hence, its political sustainability.

Somavia extended his argument to many of the remaining recommendations of the Commission. At the national level, he allied the ILO with the emphasis in the report on national measures to improve social dialogue and understand the impacts of globalization. He linked the Commission's finding to the ILO focus on national poverty reduction programs. He strongly endorsed the report's focus on global production systems, and its case for improved dialogue and global policy coherence on investment, growth and their impact on employment. The need for a social protection "floor" of standards was consistent with the ILO's own social protection focus and the intentions of the 1998 Declaration on Fundamental Principles and Rights at Work. Equally, the importance given in the report to cross-border flows of people is, argued Somavia, reflected in the ILO's work on such flows, including its relevant conventions. The report's argument that labor standards, and the opportunity for the ILO to extend their work on standards, are fundamental to any sustainable system of global governance, provided Somavia with an opportunity in his report to confirm the ILO's primacy in this area.

However, the most interesting section of the director-general's response to the Commission was his discussion of the role of the ILO in mobilizing change. How should the ILO act to promote a social dimension of globalization? He argued on three fronts: the need to mobilize the tripartite base in the ILO, its unique strength; second, the extent to which the ILO meets the transparency requirements laid down by the Commission for international agencies; third, how the ILO might change to meet the challenge of a sustainable social dimension.

On the first front, Somavia restated an important ILO credo. The social partnership and dialogue at the heart of the ILO's tripartism was a unique and powerful agency for change. If the Commission's challenges were to be met, then the ILO, using its specialist units such as the International Training Centre in Turin, was able to work with the social partners to increase their own capabilities and strengths to meet those challenges. The ILO and its social partners should also seek to build strategic alliances with civil society organizations. The ILO and the social partners were to use their understanding of inevitable change (for example, restructuring in the face of shifts in global competitiveness) to ensure that adverse effects were minimized and that positive effects were maximized.

On the second front, the transparency of the ILO's own mechanisms, Somavia suggested that "the ILO comes out reasonably well," but argued against complacency. His commentary supported that warning. He listed a number of areas in which progress might be made, for example, better evaluation and monitoring procedures, overcoming the invisibility of the ILO and its activities in the social partners' international networks, the need for better gender balance in the ILO's activities, and more citations of ILO publications in technical and academic publications.

Two concerns were particularly telling. The first was a striking admission that, whilst the ILO's conventions, and particularly the core conventions, are widely cited and are often used in CSR models, their origins in the ILO are not cited and often are unknown by those using them. This links to the second striking concern, to the effect that the ILO is "inward looking, preoccupied with procedure, relatively slow in response, and having a style of expression that deters all but the most enthusiastic from discovering our ideas." Here, Somavia was, in surprisingly candid fashion for the head of an international agency, pointing to deeply rooted internal problems within the ILO's organization, an issue addressed in more depth in the concluding chapter. He himself suggested that the ILO "might therefore be wise to reflect on how it could become more outward looking, better able to express and communicate its messages and faster in responding to demands of individual constituents, and also on the concept of tripartism itself as a tool for more effective governance." In the same vein, Somavia was willing to concede that the staff skill profile of the ILO, whilst in some areas appropriate, was in others deficient and must be addressed if the ILO is to take its rightful place on the global stage.

On the third front, the ILO, argued Somavia, had much to do to meet the challenge of a sustainable social dimension. Better capability and wider influence would allow the ILO's tripartite approach to become an important catalyst in the creation of a fair globalization. Leveraging the Commission's findings would be an important way to renew the ILO's direction and purpose, whilst consolidating the ILO at the heart of global governance. A successful social dimension of globalization would mean a successful and well-positioned ILO.

Capability development in the ILO, suggested Somavia, was needed in a number of areas. Improved analytical capacity was required in such areas as "global and national macroeconomic policy co-ordination for growth and full employment, global production systems, new integrated approaches to adjustment, social protection and labor market policies and international migration." There also remained, he noted, "numerous gaps in our understanding of the social and labor impact of global economic, financial, trade, technological and environmental policies." One option canvassed was the development and use of global research networks as a way to plug existing analytical gaps.

Other capability developments were needed in the ILO's outreach activities, where the option of wider partnerships with external stakeholders was available. Information creation and flows could be developed greatly, using the experience of the Commission's own communication and data-gathering procedures. Financial allocations might also have to be revised in the light of new priorities associated with a renewed ILO role in global governance.

The ILO and the challenge of globalization

The Commission's suggestion that there was an urgent need to build a fair and inclusive globalization, and its (and the ILO's) acceptance that globalization and market systems were givens in the global economy, set the tone for its findings and the response offered by Somavia. In one sense, this perspective could be presented as entirely consistent with ILO tradition from its founding. The ILO has not been, and indeed could not be, a radical institution, challenging the fundamental rationale of the market system. Its internal structure and processes, based on tripartism and the constructive interaction of the social partners, will not reject the market system as a principle. The status of the ILO within the broader UN system reinforced that position. The ILO was born within the capitalist system and remains firmly in that system. Its traditional role has been to challenge policy settings and outcomes within the system, in order to foster adaptation of the system. Its origins as an institution to contain revolutionary worker mobilization by providing a voice and presence in the capitalist system for workers should not be forgotten.

However, if this is the case, then has the ILO fulfilled its role as an "internal" critic of the market model? Has it, for example, been too quick to accept the logic and inevitability of globalization? Has it been able and willing to provide an effective counterpoint to the root-and-branch market fundamentalist support for globalization? Standing suggests that "[i]n the late 1980s, the ILO gained some new legitimacy—or value—for those supporting a global market society." He reasons that the ILO became a useful mechanism in support of the reintegration of the Soviet bloc into the market system. He further reasons that, as a result of strategic shifts in its focus and related events, the ILO has failed to mobilize effectively its resources and capacities against the impacts of globalization. In this, we might conclude, the ILO has not provided that counterpoint to globalization, and, by direct involvement or by omission, the ILO has been overly sympathetic to globalization and its impacts. This would, one might also conclude from Standing's analysis, lead to disaffection in the workers' camp, as they might be expected to feel the impact of globalization most immediately.

Leaving to one side for now the discussion of ILO priorities in the recent period, to which we turn in subsequent chapters, it is clear that, like many commentators and agencies, the nature and impacts of global integration were understood late in the day by the ILO. When Director-General Hansenne placed globalization firmly on the ILO agenda in 1994, it was already well-advanced in technology, financial structures, investment patterns and production systems. Moreover, its supporting macroeconomic settings ("market fundamentalism") were globally in place, having been initially introduced in the early 1970s. As we have discussed in Chapter 2, the ILO's own circumstances in the 1970s and 1980s did not help. It was threatened politically and financially by the US withdrawal, the impacts of the Cold War and other challenges. Its strategic focus for much of this period on development issues, whilst important, was deemed by some to be too narrow an agenda to comprehend the challenge posed by globalization.

As Somavia indicates explicitly, the internal operation of the ILO, inward-looking, bureaucratic, slow, and, for many inside as well as outside, impenetrable, was unlikely to drive a strongly proactive approach to globalization. The social partners were also often late in the game. Trade unions internationally understood well, for example, the impacts of market fundamentalism on jobs and investment, but were often slow to understand the level of global integration that was emerging and what its full effects might be. This was also true for employer organizations. Governments, and significant elements of the business community, were also strongly influenced by the logic of market fundamentalism, and in particular, its support for labor market flexibility, trade and investment openness, privatization and corporatization, and reductions in the size and role of the state. In this context, it was hardly likely that they would actively promote within the ILO a radical critique of globalization.

Even if the social partners had wished to move the ILO to a more critical position on globalization, and had been able to reform its internal mechanisms, there was a further challenge, that is, how to reconfigure the standards-setting approach of the ILO for the globalization era? The ILO has always seen its remit to be more than the creation of conventions and recommendations. The Declaration of Philadelphia made this clear, as does the Commission's report and the response by Somavia. But, how much more is desirable or possible? Inevitably, the search for a broader role carries with it the potential for the rethinking, or downgrading, of the importance of standard-setting, or, at least, inconsistencies and contradictions emerging between standard-setting and the broader agenda. This is a long-term challenge for the ILO, and one which it has moved to address, attracting both plaudits and criticism in the process.

Conclusion

A move from a standard-setting approach requires the development of implementation, monitoring and evaluation procedures over and above those established. This is costly, but more importantly, assumes that the ILO understands clearly what it is trying to achieve in a broader strategy, and is able to define (and measure) outcomes. The breadth of the World Commission's report highlights this challenge. Whilst praising the report, Somavia's response was careful to limit possible ILO responses, that is, he was clearly aware that a program that attempted to meet the full range of challenges raised by the Commission was well beyond the ILO's immediate mandate and capacities.

There is, however, a more pressing discussion attached to standards-setting and the ILO's responses to globalization. Alston and Heenan (2004) and Standing (2008), for example, argue that the standards-setting approach adopted by the ILO has been weakened dramatically, particularly as an effect of the 1998 Declaration of Fundamental Principles and Rights at Work. They argue, variously, that the post-1998 approach to standards has narrowed the ILO's focus to core rights, and in the process moved to a "promotional" approach to standards, rather than one grounded in firm legal obligations. They suggest that "soft" law has replaced binding law and that the traditional approach to standards as rights has been undermined. One interpretation of this undermining, opines Standing, is that it was "a small breakthrough for those wishing to see a global market society without adherence to a web of protective regulations."

To understand the changing role of standard-setting in the modern ILO, we need to understand the 1998 Declaration of Fundamental Principles and Rights at Work. It is to this we turn in the next chapter.

4 The Declaration on Fundamental Principles and Rights at Work
A new approach to labor standards?

In Chapter 3, we saw that Director-General Hansenne spoke at the 1994 International Labour Conference about the need to understand and respond to the challenges raised by globalization. We saw also how the ILO came to understand globalization, in particular in the context of the "Fair Globalisation" report. Hansenne was true to his word and vision. After 1994, he led a significant repositioning of the ILO, most notably in terms of its traditional standard-setting role, a transformation which his successor Juan Somavia has continued. At the heart of that repositioning was the 1998 Declaration on Fundamental Principles and Rights at Work (hereafter referred to as "the 1998 declaration"). In Hansenne's own words, the purpose of the repositioning was to achieve "more targeted standards for greater impact."[1]

However, for some, the 1998 declaration broke from a long-standing tradition of standard-setting within the ILO. In particular, it focused less on standards as legally binding, and more on standards as aspirational and promotional, and therefore rooted in what some see as "soft" law. Those concerned about this shift often believe that the declaration signaled a weakening of the purpose and status of the ILO. Supporters of the shift, led by Hansenne and Somavia, see the 1998 declaration and its associated priorities as an essential modernization of the ILO in the face of globalization. This chapter reviews the arguments for and against the 1998 declaration and its related impacts on the ILO.

A call for a fair globalization

The 1998 declaration in part owes its existence to a long-established concern in the ILO to extend the focus and commitment given to freedom of association by the Committee on Freedom of Association to other fundamental rights. As Hagen states explicitly,[2] the 1998 declaration was also strongly driven and supported by the employers in the

ILO. US representatives were also strongly supportive. The declaration was eventually adopted unanimously in 1998, following long and difficult debate between the social partners and ILO officials.

Hansenne's report to the 1997 International Labour Conference lays out the rationale for the 1998 declaration.[3] This rationale was clearly his, for, as in previous eras in the ILO, the 1990s called forth a director-general committed to steering the ILO in a clear direction. The argument for the 1998 declaration has three strands, two positive, one negative. The positive arguments were, believed Hansenne, the acceptance by the ILO of a need to change, manifest in ILO activities after his 1994 speech, and the support for the ILO and standard-setting in other international agencies and events, including the Copenhagen World Summit for Social Development (in which Hansenne's successor, Juan Somavia, was very active). The negative argument reflected Hansenne's concern that the consensus binding the social partners to the traditional standard-setting approach was breaking down. He saw this breakdown in the tenor and quality of debates in the ILO and believed that a new consensus must be forged in the long-term interests of the ILO. There was also, in his comments and in those of others, a concern about the effectiveness of traditional standard-setting, to which we return below.

In an important continuity with previous activist directors-general, there is in Hansenne's speeches an explicit sense of globalization as an opportunity for the ILO. This opportunity derives from the corollary of unfettered globalization, global governance. As global economic integration proceeds, so will arise the need for effective global regulation, and in matters relating to labor and work, and what they mean for human dignity and rights, the ILO will reinforce and extend its role as the source of standards and, importantly, values. There is also another striking theme in his analysis, to the effect that labor standards have little purpose in themselves, but are a means to achieve desirable outcomes in work and life. It follows from this that the delivery of the standards message must be attuned to the prevailing economic and social circumstances. Traditional ways of thinking about and implementing standards may no longer be appropriate

In his report to the 1997 International Labour Conference, Hansenne argued that the ILO could work in two interdependent ways in order to maximize its impact. The first was in achieving "universal recognition of certain basic rights which should allow the social partners to claim their legitimate share in the development resulting from globalization—which may therefore be viewed as the 'social rules of the game of globalization.'" Here, Hansenne took a big stride away from traditional ILO thinking. This was the rationale for the specification of "core" labor standards. Drawing on outcomes and discussions in the WTO, the OECD and in the World Summit for Social Development, particularly related to standards and the multilateral trade system, he developed further a view found in those discussions. This identified core labor standards as not only able to guarantee fundamental rights, but, also, able so to do in a context in which "any fears that the application of these standards might influence the competitive positioning of these countries in the context of liberalization are unfounded." Thus, we arrive at the notion of core labor standards, which, when applied, simultaneously meet the requirements of the market and of human rights and dignity.

The second way proposed "the setting up of an appropriate institutional framework to encourage States to use any benefits they might reap from globalization for achieving social progress." In its simplest form, this would involve the ILO working with member states to encourage them to integrate a social dimension into their economic strategies, particularly by the adoption of labor standards. The mechanisms for this were twofold, first, emulation, whereby the ILO would support technically in each state the extension of a social dimension from a minimum provision to something more, using ILO conventions as a means.

Second, social labeling (later often described as "the overall social label," and possibly based on a new convention) involved "an entirely voluntary and multilateral system for mutual recognition of social labels between States which could cover all or some of their export products, depending on the wishes of the States themselves" and also a variety of codes of conduct. Simply, the idea was that products produced on the basis of good labor standards would be labeled as such, and might gain a premium in the marketplace, thus encouraging further adoption of standards. Hansenne later backed away from this approach as concerns emerged within the ILO, especially on the part of developing countries, that social labeling might be a proxy for protectionism. Hansenne also highlighted the role of non-government actors, whereby the ILO might work with the growing number of significant NGOs to advance the social dimension. The emulation and social labeling suggestions represented significant shifts away from the traditional standard-setting approach of the ILO.

Hansenne provided a blueprint of a refocused, "modernized" ILO in which core standards particularly address fundamental rights, and the ILO develops strategies to encourage member states to emulate good practice, and in which it builds alliances with NGOs in member states, both with the intention of extending the social dimension. To complement this refocusing, Hansenne proposed that standards should be better targeted for greater impact. The argument for better targeting was driven by emerging circumstances: first, the possibility that globalization would lead to an increase in the number of opportunities for standard-setting; second, diminishing returns to standards might result from this; third, there were other standard-setting agencies also producing standards, which might lead to a "standards overload" in member states. Hansenne was suggesting, therefore, that the traditional ILO process of standard-setting had to change if ILO standards were to be ratified and observed. There was an internal political issue also in Hansenne's mind. The ILO's internal consensus around standard-setting was beginning to fray at the edges as the social partners began to question the substance and purpose of possible new standards. Hence, the idea of fewer, better structured, targeted standards, with greater impact and support, was attractive to the ILO leadership.

How would a more streamlined standard-setting model work? It would require a more strategic, and less ad hoc, approach to deciding what standards should be developed. This would require better consultation from the beginning with the social partners. Standards set in place should be assessed against their "value add." The ILO should be "looking for standards with the highest 'added value.'" The ILO might think of rationalizing the existing standards, which sometimes overlap, or are outdated. Existing standards might be "codified," providing an opportunity for standards involving general and important principles to be differentiated from those with a specific, narrower remit. The ILO should also recognize that specific standards might better be complemented or replaced by statements of principle (principles of responsibility), where the rate of change in work circumstances is so great that the prospect of multiple standards arises. Standards should be better drafted, clearer in intended effect, not subject to significant, frequent amendment, and should be subject to review (and possible revision). The issue of evaluation of standards, and their possible revision, was an important feature of Hansenne's refocusing of the standard-setting process. Here, and elsewhere in his thinking, it is possible to discern in Hansenne a sympathy for performance management techniques, and for greater efficiency and effectiveness in the work of the ILO. Undoubtedly, this also reflected a concern about the inner workings of the ILO as an organization, and a recognition that a refocusing of the standard-setting model would have important implications for its structure and operations.

Hansenne also suggested that standards-related discussion should be distanced from more general, topical discussion in the ILO. No doubt, this was intended to limit the "automatic" response to consider a new standard whenever an issue was raised. Critics might interpret that distancing of standard-setting from general discussion as downplaying of the standard-setting process. His comments on recommendations and conventions might reinforce this concern. Conventions are, of course, promulgated to be translated into member states' legal systems. They are intended to create legal obligations. Recommendations are simply that: non-mandatory suggestions about how member states should act in a particular context.

Drawing on debate in the ILO over many years, Hansenne strongly endorsed the view that recommendations should no longer be the poor relations of conventions. He made a strong argument that recommendations are often as successful as conventions, especially as the latter may not be ratified, and, if they are, may not be observed in practice. In making this argument, he risked the wrath of the workers' group in the ILO, which traditionally argued that conventions, even those still unratified, were powerful signals to member states. The suggestion was that, normally, recommendations should become "autonomous," that is, not dependent on a convention, but free-standing, and that their impact should be assessed and promoted by regular reporting and follow-up activities in the ILO. Hansenne was, it might reasonably be argued, promoting an upgrading of recommendations, not a downgrading of conventions, but some would see this differently.

This, then, was the blueprint for a refocused, modernized ILO. Its traditional core work (standard-setting) would be restructured to become better targeted and evaluated, involving a clear distinction between core, fundamental standards, and others, and an upgrading of the role of recommendations. Central to the proposal was a detailed follow-up to its adoption, including a system of regular reporting, including annual reviews of the 1998 declaration and the production of an annual global report on, in any given year, one of the fundamental rights.

The subsequent developments in the ILO between 1997 and 1998 were the stuff of classical international organization politics.[4] The 1998 Declaration on Fundamental Principles and Rights at Work was to be the vehicle for this modernization agenda and it had to be taken through constitutional procedures and be accepted by the International Labour Conference. Thus, between November 1997 and June 1998, a series of consultations took place across the ILO and its social partners. The purpose was to allay fears about the proposed refocusing and develop a draft declaration, which could be taken to the June 1998 International Labour Conference. These consultations were, in diplomatic terms, frank. All three parties had concerns about the rationale for the change. For example, some governments objected to any suggestion that the ILO should be able to dictate the rate of social progress in member states. Many parties were confused by and concerned about the "overall social label" approach. Many workers were fearful of a reduction in the importance of legally binding standard-setting. Hansenne's argument about support for his proposed changes derived from, for example, the Copenhagen Social Summit, was disputed. The constitutional status of a declaration created difficulties for some. For example, was it legally binding? Others were exercised by the impact of a declaration. Would be it be used effectively beyond the ILO as part of a comprehensive standards-building process, or would it be seen as ineffectual and therefore weaken the status of the ILO? What the promulgation of a declaration would mean for the organization of the ILO and for the social partners' rights and responsibilities was also addressed in the consultation process.

Notwithstanding the frankness of the debate and the range of issues raised by the social partners, in June 1998 the International Labour Conference adopted unanimously the Declaration on Fundamental Principles and Rights at Work at its 86th session. The final wording of the 1998 declaration is concise and may be reduced to four key elements.[5] First, the declaration confirms that, by joining the ILO, and endorsing the principles set out in the ILO's constitution and the Declaration of Philadelphia, member states are bound by the principles related to four fundamental areas of rights, which are:

(a) freedom of association and the effective recognition of the right to collective bargaining;
(b) the elimination of all forms of forced or compulsory labor;
(c) the effective abolition of child labor; and
(d) the elimination of discrimination in respect of employment and occupation.

Second, member states and the ILO, working together with other agencies, will support these fundamental rights:

(a) by offering technical co-operation and advisory services to promote the ratification and implementation of the fundamental conventions;
(b) by assisting those members not yet in a position to ratify some or all of these conventions in their efforts to respect, to promote and to realize the principles concerning fundamental rights which are the subject of those conventions; and
(c) by helping the members in their efforts to create a climate for economic and social development.

Third, the 1998 declaration will be promoted by means of an annual "follow-up" at member-state level in cases where one or more of the four fundamental areas have not been addressed appropriately in terms of convention ratification, and an annual "global report," analyzing one of the fundamental rights each year. Fourth, labor standards should not be used for protectionist purposes.

The performance of the 1998 declaration is reported principally in three ways: director-general reports to the International Labour Conference, the global report is presaged in the declaration, and in the proposed follow-up activity, reported to the Governing Body. Thus, for example, in 2008, in his report to the 97th International Labour Conference on ILO implementation, Director-General Somavia outlined the ILO's achievements in relation to its Strategic Objective 1, that is, "to promote and realize standards and fundamental principles at work."[6] He reported an expenditure of US$233.7 million and a "strong" role for labor standards, measured by reference to standards across financial institutions, UN initiatives, private sector activities and codes of conduct. The role included significant technical assistance opportunities for the ILO. Performance is then broken down into constituent areas, each with an actual outcome reported against a target outcome. Thus, for example, the proposed outcome covering the improved implementation of fundamental principles and rights at work is assessed by six indicators, in five of which targets were exceeded. The indicators include categories such as "Constituents use tools and other practical measures to implement fundamental principles and rights at work," "Member States take action for improved respect for freedom of association and effective recognition of the right to collective bargaining" and "Tripartite constituents are more capable of promoting freedom of association and collective bargaining; social partners have greater capacity to organize the unorganized." The overall message from this annual report is that the work driven by the 1998 declaration is successful.

The global report is similarly positive. Whilst each annual report takes up one of the areas of fundamental rights, the 2008 Report, reflecting on the decade since the adoption of the 1998 declaration, provides some overview data on the take-up of those fundamental rights over that period. In terms of the subject of the 2008 Report, freedom of association, it notes a 44 percent increase in ratifications of Convention 98 and a 64 percent increase in the case of Convention 87 between 1990 and 2007. The increase since 1998, when the declaration was introduced, was smaller in the case of Convention 98, where 60 percent of the increase came in the 1990–97 period, but larger in the case of Convention 87, for which the corresponding figure is 48 percent. It is noteworthy that the Report makes little of the impact of the declaration in its reporting of figures. For example, there are interesting data on the take-up of all the fundamental conventions, yet the reporting period is 1995 to 2007. The year 1995 is chosen, notes the Report, because that was the year that the campaign in support of ratification of fundamental conventions was initiated (following the Copenhagen Global Summit). Despite the global report's status as a deliverable related to the declaration, the substantive effect of the declaration is not explored in any significant detail. Its impact is suggested by association with the broader data provided.

The "follow-up" process involving the Governing Body was initiated in 1999. It is in the detail of the follow-up that the promotional dimensions of the 1998 declaration become particularly clear. The follow-up process is "strictly promotional" and is designed to encourage member states to promote fundamental rights, using the technical assistance offered by the ILO. Employer representatives strongly support this approach. The survey forms circulated in relation to the follow-up are much in tune with the approach of encouragement and promotion. In 2000, the Governing Body received its first follow-up studies. Taking advice from a group of expert advisers, it focused on promotional activities, technical assistance, information flows and the like as a response to those studies. This has been the tenor of the follow-up since 2000. The follow-up mechanism is not designed to provide an assessment of the effectiveness of the declaration.

The Declaration on Fundamental Principles and Rights at Work and ILO strategy

The 1998 declaration was an important refocusing of the ILO's activities. In line with previous strategic positioning of the ILO, it was driven by the then director-general, in this case with strong support from the employer group (to the point that Hagen describes it as an employer initiative).[7] The declaration was designed to equip the ILO to respond to the challenges of globalization, building on traditional strengths in standard-setting and technical assistance, but targeting efforts to greater effect and putting greater energy into the promotion and resourcing of standards in member states. It was, as we noted, passed unanimously, but only after complex and often heated debate within the ILO. ILO assessments of its effects are broadly positive.

Notwithstanding that unanimity and a widespread agreement that the ILO needed to refocus its activities to meet the challenges of globalization, the 1998 declaration is shrouded in controversy. Critics regard it as at best a weak alternative to the traditional standard-setting approach and, at worst, a betrayal of that approach and a capitulation

54 *A new approach to labor standards?*

to the forces for globalization. For the critics, it has become a key symbol of all that is wrong with the modern ILO.

What are the essential criticisms offered of the 1998 declaration?[8] First, there is the argument that, in practice, it shores up the market fundamentalist approach underpinning globalization. In this view, the declaration undermined the debate around the inclusion of a social clause in trade deals by diverting attention and effort elsewhere (see Chapters 5 and 6 for further discussion). The four fundamental areas do not constitute a strategy to respond to globalization, as they are "negative rights," already covered in most jurisdictions by common law. They are, runs this argument, areas to which member states can pay lip-service without engaging seriously with more pressing and difficult issues. In any case, the declaration simply seeks the promotion and resourcing of these areas, hoping that effective change follows from those activities, but without any redress if such change does not happen. Finally, the 1998 declaration creates a ceiling rather than a floor of standards, hamstringing the ILO's ability to contribute to the creation of global justice.[9]

This leads to a second important criticism. The traditional strength of the ILO standard-setting system was the translation of conventions into law, creating legally binding outcomes in member states. Critics bemoan the shift embodied in the 1998 declaration from "hard" law to "soft" law, from enactment to promotion. That shift, runs the criticism, also moves the ILO debate significantly away from rights to broad principles, with the latter much more difficult to implement than rights associated with enforceable conventions.

Third, the focus in the 1998 declaration on negative rights also marginalizes important economic rights (employment security, pensions, maternity benefits, etc.) which traditionally would have had something akin to equal status with the declaration's core rights. Underpinning this argument is a belief that the body of rights traditionally encompassed by the ILO was indivisible and provided a coherent framework for social justice. That coherence, and therefore the impact of the ILO, has been fundamentally compromised by the prioritization of core rights adopted in the declaration.

Fourth, the approach adopted by the 1998 declaration permits responsibility for standards to devolve on a voluntary basis to the private sector and other agencies. This argument has three strands. The first believes that this devolution, when coupled with the shift from hard to soft law, will be at best partial and much less effective in establishing standards than the traditional ILO process, Second, by devolving standard-setting to the private sector on a voluntary basis, the ILO is ceding important ground to initiatives such as Corporate

A new approach to labor standards? 55

Social Responsibility (CSR), which are top-down, managerial strategies lacking many of the social justice dimensions of the traditional ILO model. Critics believe that reference to ILO conventions in such initiatives is a poor alternative to traditional standard-setting. Third, heterogeneous standard-setting across multiple agencies and locations will be confused and will undermine the creation of a single, coherent and effective international standards framework.

Fifth, the evidence for the success of the 1998 declaration is not strong. The reporting process associated with the declaration is self-serving and lightweight. Rigorous assessment would probably show the impact of the declaration to be at best minimal.

Sixth, the 1998 declaration reflects a politically contingent approach by the ILO to the challenges it faced as a result of globalization. The subtext here is that market fundamentalism had eroded employer and government commitment to traditional tripartism and the ILO model. This explained the growing difficulty in establishing consensus around new conventions in the ILO. To preserve the ILO and reassert a new consensus, the ILO has eroded its focus on a coherent, universal framework of labor standards, leaving it in a weak position. Moreover, there is no guarantee that the new accommodation will be sustainable. The ILO may lose its status as primus inter pares in global labor standard-setting and, in time, become irrelevant. In this argument, the mechanism adopted to save the ILO may, in fact, be its nemesis.

Criticisms of the 1998 declaration have drawn a detailed response from the senior ranks of the ILO.[10] The core of Maupain's counter-argument is that, first, the declaration has been effective, that is, the supposed disadvantages associated with a move from the traditional ILO model to the framework imposed by the declaration can be shown empirically not to exist. Second, to the extent that constraints exist on the ILO after the adoption of the declaration, those constraints were already a feature of the traditional model. Moreover, the critique of the declaration is rejected as polemical, methodologically unsound and, also unbalanced, for it takes the declaration out of the broader operation of the ILO in which it functions.

The methodological question is an appropriate starting point for discussion. When the critics argue for a traditional standard-setting approach, rather than a new, declaration-based approach, do they address the old and the new in commensurate terms? Or do they fail to note the true nature and depth of the challenges facing the traditional model, and thus skew their analysis against the new? Maupain argues that balance is not achieved in the critique and, implicitly, that, if it were, the outcome of the critique might be different.

Maupain then turns to the nature of the change brought about by the 1998 declaration. His purpose is to shift the point of discussion from a concern about how radical a refocusing has taken place to how effective it has been in practice. In doing so, Maupain is invoking analytical order in the face of an implied polemical inconsistency. Thus, the declaration is a "decisive departure" from a pick-and-choose model of compliance with standards to one in which ILO membership demands substantive commitment to core values. Moreover, this is an extension of pre-1998 practice around Freedom of Association, in place since 1950. The development of the declaration took into account the experience of the Freedom of Association complaints process, wherein a complaints-based or "name and shame" approach to enforcement developed. This is precisely why the promotion and encouragement model was adopted in the declaration, for governments would never accept the extension of the name and shame model to other areas of ILO. Moreover, there is nothing necessarily weaker about the follow-up process adopted for the declaration. The chosen approach allows issues to be identified, technical resources to be deployed and extended dialogue to take place, which together provide a powerful mechanism for change.

The idea that the 1998 declaration is a contingent political accommodation which arbitrarily limits the role of the ILO by differentiating core from other standards is also assailed by Maupain. His argument is, in simple terms, all accommodations in the ILO are political. It is the nature of the beast and should surprise no-one. The declaration does not create a hierarchy amongst standards, in that core status does not create in any constitutional fashion a second tier of standards, and the particular identification of specific standards at a given point in history is not new to the ILO. In addition, the areas of fundamental rights identified in the declaration are both functionally and analytically integrated and do, directly and indirectly, relate to economic rights.

The counter-response addresses the rights versus principles debate. There is, argues Maupain, no chance that the principles in the 1998 declaration will become independent of the underpinning conventions (rights), that is, the declaration is in this context firmly rooted in the traditional practices and expectations of the ILO. That rooting also should allay concerns that the ILO, by adopting the declaration, is contributing to heterogeneity (that is, standard-setting by other agencies) in standard-setting. That heterogeneity was already in place before the declaration. Also rejected is the argument that the specificity, and, therefore, effectiveness, associated with the traditional standards-based model, will somehow be lost as an effect of the adoption of broad principles.

Finally, the counter-response provides empirical material seeking to support the argument that the 1998 declaration has had a positive impact in terms of member state initiatives and understanding, and ratification of fundamental conventions. Also proposed is the capacity of the reporting process associated with the declaration to adapt and improve.

Support for the 1998 declaration and Hansenne's strategic redirection of the ILO comes not only from within the ILO. Langille, for example, suggests that the Alston critique is misguided and misses the point of the reform.[11] To start with, Langille suggests that Alston might have begun his analysis of the declaration by asking simple, sensible questions. Were the changes right? Did they benefit working people? Instead of engaging consistently and robustly with the changes and assessing their impact, Alston, argues Langille, might also have contrasted what preceded the declaration with what followed, thus making an informed comparative assessment.

However, Langille is more concerned about a misguided focus on the adverse effects of the 1998 declaration on what Alston identified to be the heart of the ILO, the traditional labor rights regime. Langille argues that this misguided focus lies in the thesis, evident in both Alston and Standing, that the ILO has weakened its defense of labor rights as an effect of globalization and its ideology, neo-liberalism. The declaration was, in Alston's view, a way of subverting the ILO in line with the needs of globalization, whilst simultaneously making use of the ILO as a useful facade behind which globalization would prosper. For Langille, this is a "deeply shallow understanding" of the role of the ILO and the problems that it addresses. That understanding is, believes Langille, flawed in many ways. To begin with, it misrepresents the status and role of the ILO and its focus on labor rights. By overstating the international significance and priority of the ILO and its rights activities, Alston's thesis overstates the adverse impact of the declaration. Moreover, suggests Langille, it misunderstands the position of the ILO before and after the declaration; one of many institutions and agencies, actors and interventions addressing international labor law, important, perhaps paramount, but not unique. Hence, the status of the ILO has not precipitately declined as an effect of the declaration, nor has the international focus on international labor law been undermined, and nor has the range of agencies and institutions concerned about labor law grown in ways that threaten the value of what the ILO does.

Langille has other concerns about criticisms of the 1998 declaration. It does not, he suggests, weaken the ILO by downgrading the importance of labor rights, but improves its positioning in terms of emerging debates such as those around the Social Clause and WTO. The declaration should not be judged against putative motivations attributed to people, but against what it achieves. There is no weakening of the rights focus in the ILO by the introduction of the notion of principles, rather a legitimate shift from standards to rights in the grammar and focus of the ILO. Alston has, suggests Langille, misunderstood the rights-principles and enforcement-promotion relationships involved in the declaration.

Langille argues that, in multiple ways, the contrast provided by Alston between pre- and post-declaration ILOs is inaccurate. For example, Langille argues that a move from precision in conventions to a broader statement of principles was necessary in order to make ILO measures telling across very different social and cultural contexts. Indeed, the declaration involves an approach more likely to achieve labor rights in member states. It is also a move that confronts the growing crisis in the ILO around standard-setting and supervision, a crisis manifest in declining rates of ratification and difficulties in supervising compliance. Langille makes a stronger point still: Alston's belief that in "detailed law and its enforcement" was to be found the alternative to the declaration approach is fundamentally wrong, for that was not how the ILO had traditionally achieved success. Enforcement was never the key weapon at the ILO's disposal. Engagement, promotion and persuasion were, argues Langille, the mainstays of the ILO armory.

Langille's concerns continue. Why, he mused, does Alston not address the coherence, or otherwise, of the idea of core labor rights, on which the 1998 declaration rests? Here lies the crux of Langille's concern. At the risk of over-simplifying a complex argument, Langille accuses Alston of failing to understand the purpose of the declaration in its goal, and the ILO's traditional goal, to support the establishment of both procedural rights and substantive standards, that is, mechanisms whereby outcomes are defined, and what the "floor" of outcomes should be. In particular, the definition of core rights in the declaration is conceptually coherent and central to the sustaining of employee voice in the work context. The definition of these particular core rights in the declaration, argues Langille, also promotes respect for non-core rights, for substantive rights follow the successful implementation of procedural rights. In sum, Langille is presenting a powerful case, not just for a successful modernization of the ILO and its standard-setting regime, but also for far better focus in, and outcomes from, that standard-setting.

Conclusion

The debate about the ILO's refocusing around the 1998 declaration is robust and is still to be concluded. On the face of things, it might look like there are some points of contact between the two positions, but closer examination suggests that there is a battle joined for the future of the ILO as an organization and for effective labor standards in which the declaration is a major point of engagement. We consider the debate in terms of three issues: the rationale for action, the action adopted, and the effect and effectiveness of the action. Everyone agrees that there was a need for action, but there are differences in substance and emphasis in the explanation of that need. Hansenne's rationale for change is quite measured. The challenge of globalization must be addressed, the social partners in the ILO understand this, external agencies are promoting the need for an effective ILO response, and, in any case, the internal consensus in the ILO needs to be reconstituted if labor standards are to play a role in the new global economy. The critics' analysis agrees that globalization must be engaged. However, the ILO has, according to their argument, arrived at this conclusion late in the day after a long period of uncertainty about its role and effectiveness. The manner of its arrival at the need for action has not only weakened the resolve of the ILO to act in traditional defense of labor standards, but also brought the ILO substantially in line with market fundamentalist perspectives.

The action adopted therefore takes on two competing personas. From the "official" perspective, the 1998 declaration is an effective way to refocus the standards process, which finds unanimity in the ILO and has been shown to work well. The new system draws on the old, yet also adapts it to deal with the new realities of globalization. Criticisms of the declaration and the new approach, argue the pro-reform tradition, are grounded in polemic, misunderstanding and misrepresentation. However, from the critics' perspective, the new approach loses much of the quality and leverage that the traditional standards model enjoyed, distances unacceptably the conventions from the four fundamental areas of rights, relies on ineffectual promotion and encouragement, and meets the needs of employers and some governments willing to see a compliance-based ILO model debilitated.

The "official" view is that the reporting channels associated with the declaration suggest that it is working well. Critics suggest the new approach has not been shown to be successful and that it is probably more likely to do long-term damage. In sum, the former view is convinced that the ILO has, once more, skillfully repositioned itself in the face of global shifts. The latter is deeply concerned that the strength of the ILO has been dissipated and that the future of standard-setting is at risk.

The critics, beyond their dark warnings, also propose an alternative, which may still be possible. The alternative involves, amongst other things, a re-rooting of the new model in the traditional conventions-based approach, tied to improved follow-up and monitoring of activities. It also may require internal renovation of the ILO organization, its skill base and, possibly, the addressing of some other long-term issues, such as how representative the employer and worker groups in the ILO are. In other words, the debates around globalization and the declaration pose fundamental questions about the viability of the ILO as the center of the global labor standards process. It is a theme to which we return later. However, notwithstanding the criticisms of the declaration, reform of the ILO was successfully begun by Hansenne. It was to be taken forward by his successor, Juan Somavia, in dynamic fashion. We turn to the Somavia years in Chapter 6. In Chapter 5, we address one of the most complex and contentious issues to assail the ILO in recent history, the potential for a link between labor standards and the WTO's trade regime.

5 The ILO and the WTO
The tortuous case of the Social Clause

More than a decade before the 1998 Declaration of Fundamental Principles and Rights at Work, the question of "core" or "fundamental" labor standards had surfaced in another context. As the 1986–94 Uruguay Round of the General Agreement on Tariffs and Trade (GATT) moved ponderously to its conclusion in Marrakesh, and on to the creation of the World Trade Organization in 1995, the question of a possible link between trade arrangements and labor standards arose. Specifically, the suggestion emerged within the GATT negotiations that countries seeking the advantages of free trade under GATT rules should set in place a platform of minimum labor standards. If not, they should be penalized by losing some of the trade advantages offered by GATT arrangements. The rationale for the proposal was the promotion of a "race to the top" in terms of labor standards and production systems, rather than a "race to the bottom," in which countries competed on the basis of cheapness of their labor.

The proposed provision was widely known as the "Social Clause." The proposal polarized opinion amongst countries negotiating the GATT round, particularly between developed countries in the North and developing countries in the South. Moreover, it split the international trade union movement between supporters (mainly developed economy unions) and opponents (mainly developing country unions). It also placed labor standards, and therefore the ILO, at the heart of one of the major economic debates of the period. For the ILO, it raised the questions about the nature and identification of core standards, the ILO's engagement with other international agencies and procedures, and its capacity to be a big league player in the globalization process. The ILO's stance on the trade–labor standards linkage became an important element in Hansenne's refocusing of the ILO.

A polarized debate

The invocation of a Social Clause, or something similar, was not new. For example, the idea that labor conditions might be unfair, and therefore, a possible distorting factor in international trade, was recognized in the Havana Charter of the stillborn International Trade Organization (ITO) in 1947. The Brandt Commission, reporting in 1980, called for internationally agreed "fair" labor standards to "prevent unfair competition and facilitate trade liberalization," while the European Commission supported the concept of a GATT social clause in 1986. The United States has long maintained a range of legislation and practices permitting labor standards to be taken into account in trade arrangements, most notably in its General System of Preferences (GSP), which allows the US president to withdraw trade advantages from a country which does not offer internationally recognized workers' rights. The North American Free Trade Agreement (NAFTA) has had a "side agreement" (the North American Agreement on Labor Cooperation, NAALC) in place since 1994. The United States was to the fore in the Uruguay Round debate on a social clause, calling for its inclusion from 1986. Some international commodity agreements also make reference to labor standards. As a final example, in 1994, the European Union introduced measures offering more GSP benefits to countries which have core labor standards in place, and fewer benefits to those which do not.

The generic Social Clause proposal identified seven core conventions, which would be linked to trade arrangements.[1] How the Social Clause would work was the subject of extensive debate. Options included the use of raised tariffs, restricted quotas, exclusion from preferential trading benefits (GSP provisions or those associated with Most Favored Nation status), or complete closure of some or all trade links for a period or indefinitely. How it might be incorporated into the rules of the WTO after 1995 was a complex discussion, which, in the event, was never required to be resolved (see below).

The Social Clause also polarized the economic debate about trade and growth between market fundamentalists, who, generally, opposed any linkage of trade and labor standards, and others, who supported the linkage.[2] Interesting though the technical debate on the economic effects of the linkage is, its political fall-out is particularly important. At the level of the nation-state, the debate created divisions between developing and developed economies. Much as in the debate around environmental issues, developing economies observed a barely hidden protectionism in the push for a trade–labor standards linkage.

Countries such as India and Malaysia were strong opponents of the linkage. Employers and trade unions in developing countries often opposed the linkage because of a fear of protectionism and increased compliance requirements. On the other side, France, the United States and the Scandinavian countries were clearly for the linkage, as was the International Confederation of Free Trade Unions (ICFTU) and the developed world's union movement.

That clash emerged wherever the debate about standards took place, including in the ILO. It is for this reason that the 1998 Declaration of Fundamental Principles and Rights at Work[3] includes the phrase, drawn from the WTO Singapore Declaration,

> that labor standards should not be used for protectionist trade purposes, and that nothing in this Declaration and its follow-up shall be invoked or otherwise used for such purposes; in addition, the comparative advantage of any country should in no way be called into question by this Declaration and its follow-up.

This is also an important factor in the ILO's contemporary approach to standard-setting. Traditionally, the expectation was that conventions should be adopted in member states as a "floor" of standards. In practice, countries could pick and choose which conventions they ratified. Conventions and recommendations were also worded flexibly to allow implementation in many different circumstances. However, the goal was to extend social justice into labor markets and wider social provision globally by means of ratified conventions. Under the declaration and the outcome of the trade–labor standards debate outlined below, the idea of a universal floor of standards, accruing over time at different speeds and in different configurations, depending on the country, has given way to a more contingent model of countries being encouraged to engage with the four fundamental areas of rights at their own speed, with the full weight of moral suasion that existed under the traditional standards model still in place, but with less emphasis on the enforcement dimension. The opposition of developing countries to "externally imposed" standards was a factor in the move toward the promotion and encouragement model at the heart of Hansenne's strategic shift in ILO focus in the 1990s. Promotion and encouragement recognizes flexibility in the pace and scope of standard-setting, appropriate to different stages in development. Employer support for the declaration reflected employer preferences for promotion and encouragement, and opposition to any rules-based approach.

A brief history of the Social Clause

The United States raised the issue of a trade–labor standards linkage when the Uruguay Round began in 1986. Whilst the proposal received some support, particularly from some countries in the North, it gained little traction in what became ever more complex technical trade negotiations, dealing for the first time with issues such as services and intellectual property. The United States raised the idea throughout the trade negotiations, but there was little energy in the GATT process to prioritize it. In a response that would become the WTO's default position, the Social Clause was sidelined as a non-trade issue. At the Marrakesh meeting in 1994, which wrapped up the Uruguay Round, the Social Clause, though discussed, was a marginal issue, left in the category of non-trade issues possibly to be addressed by the Preparatory Committee for the WTO. This contrasted with another trade-linked issue, the environment, for which a special committee was established

However, notwithstanding its marginalization in the Uruguay Round, the Social Clause continued to be an issue in the WTO. At the conclusion of negotiations, some governments (the United States and France, for example) wished to see the issue given prominence, as did the ICFTU. The first ministerial meeting of the WTO, in Singapore in 1996, provided the first formal context in which the Social Clause would be raised again in the WTO process. From an ILO perspective, Singapore was notable for the sudden withdrawal of an invitation to ILO director-general Hansenne to speak, apparently a result of some countries, primarily from the developing world, refusing to discuss trade and labor issues in the WTO. The ILO's Governing Body noted that the observer status of the ILO representative "lent particular eloquence to its (the ILO's) enforced silence."[4]

Attempts to make the trade–labor standards linkage by means of a Social Clause were unsuccessful at the Singapore meeting. The WTO was prepared to support the observance of core labor standards, but was not prepared to see those standards enforced by trade sanctions. The emerging consensus in the WTO sustained the view that labor standards were not a trade issue, and should be the responsibility of the ILO. Collaboration between the ILO and the WTO was supported, albeit in an undefined way. The final declaration of the Singapore meeting included a paragraph, presumably intended to lay out definitively the WTO perspective on the Social Clause. It read:

> We renew our commitment to the observance of internationally recognized core labor standards. The International Labour Organization (ILO) is the competent body to set and deal with these

standards, and we affirm our support for its work in promoting them. We believe that economic growth and development fostered by increased trade and further trade liberalization contribute to the promotion of these standards. We reject the use of labor standards for protectionist purposes, and agree that the comparative advantage of countries, particularly low-wage developing countries, must in no way be put into question. In this regard, we note that the WTO and ILO Secretariats will continue their existing collaboration.[5]

The product of some political intrigue and backroom discussion, this statement served to keep the Social Clause debate simmering. Its reference to the observance of internationally recognized core labor standards gave hope to some that the issue was not dead within the WTO.

The statement also provided the ILO with an opportunity to consolidate categorically its responsibility for labor standards in the global economy, for it coincided with Hansenne's 1994 challenge to the ILO to understand and act on the impact of globalization (see Chapters 3 and 4). It emphasized the process wherein the ILO became more actively engaged with other international agencies on the global stage, to be prioritized by Somavia when he became ILO director-general in 1999.

The WTO ministers gathered again in Geneva in 1998. Circumstances contrived to make social protection an important international issue as the meeting convened. The financial crisis of the late 1990s had taken a firm grip of economies in Asia, and there were growing fears that its contagion would spread into Latin America and Russia, and beyond. In this context, a narrow trade focus in the WTO was more difficult to sustain as expectations grew about the WTO's contribution to solving the international financial crisis. Ministers once again affirmed the WTO's support for core labor principles and accepted a US-EU proposal to the effect that a joint WTO-ILO forum be convened. Once again, the WTO had not been able to quash the issue. Equally, however, hard-line opposition to a trade–labor standards linkage remained within the WTO. Clouding and complicating the issue was the emergence of the United Nations' Global Compact as another important initiative in which the promotion of labor standards played a part. Opponents of the trade–standards link could point to the Global Compact and the ILO as powerful, independent proponents of labor standards who should be responsible for that work, leaving the WTO to its own trade-specific responsibilities.

Its Seattle 2000 ministerial meeting was a debacle for the WTO. It was notable for massive civil mobilization against the WTO agenda, and the emergence of insurmountable developing country dissatisfaction with trade negotiations. Above all, President Clinton, in the throes of an election campaign, but also in line with established US positions, raised a strident voice on labor issues. He pushed, with the European Union, for the joint activity between the ILO and the WTO presaged in Geneva. Many developing countries, already exercised about the WTO itself, and in particular about developed-economy domination of its outcomes, were incensed by this renewed focus on the trade–labor standards linkage. Accusations of US protectionism were common. For supporters of the linkage, Seattle may have been a pyrrhic victory. The issue may have been given prominence, but it also became openly and heatedly divisive. The WTO is a consensus-based organization, and consensus would be needed for the linkage to make ground in WTO discussions. Consensus on the linkage, already a remote prospect, was further damaged by the polarization that occurred in Seattle.

In this context, it is not surprising that the Doha WTO meeting in 2001 simply revisited ground covered in the Singapore meeting. There was no will in the WTO to take the trade–standards linkage further. Complexities in the trade agenda compounded this lack of will. Developing and transitional countries were now about 80 percent of the membership of the WTO and were increasingly challenging the developed countries grip on the WTO. General support for the linkage to trade was less likely than ever.

The Doha meeting, and the subsequent travails associated with the Doha Development Round, have ensured that the Social Clause debate is moribund. ILO-WTO discussions continue, in part as a result of Somavia's opening of the ILO to contact with other international agencies (see Chapter 6), and as a follow-up to the WTO commitment to maintain links with the ILO. The most significant outcome of those links is the 2007 joint WTO-ILO report on trade and employment.[6] This is an interesting study of the social and labor market effects of trade adjustments, concluding that there is a strong interaction between trade policy and its social and labor market counterparts. The follow-up to this report placed the ILO firmly in its traditional social protection and labor market role, and did not in any way envisage a renewal of the Social Clause approach.[7] Further collaboration with the WTO was envisaged, but clearly at the level of joint studies. For those with high hopes of an enforceable link between core labor standards and trade, it was a modest return to 20 years of campaigning.

The Social Clause and the ILO

In Chapter 4, we discussed how the 1998 Declaration on Fundamental Principles and Rights at Work moved the ILO from a focus on conventions enforced in domestic law to a promotional and encouragement-based focus in which fundamental areas of rights were advocated in member states. Hansenne applied this perspective as much to trade-related matters as he did to labor standards. He argued in 1994 that, while the demand for social justice and action on social inequalities was driven by the consequences of globalization, the ILO "should not advocate either restrictions on trade or a compulsory equalization of social costs."[8] This view was developed further in his argument for the declaration.[9] Hansenne reflected on the heated and deadlocked debate in the Working Party on the Social Dimensions of the Liberalization of International Trade, established in the ILO in 1994 to explore standard-setting and the international trade system. The Working Party had been the site of major disagreements, primarily around the desirability of a trade–labor standards link and what the role of the ILO should be in trade-related issues. Hansenne chose to take a positive out of those disagreements, to the effect that trade issues and the goals of the ILO are interdependent, and argued, "lifting restrictions on international trade lays the foundations for social progress—as the ILO has always implicitly acknowledged, even during the worst years of economic depression." Moreover, he explicitly argued that the ILO is vital for the multilateral trade system, not because its activities will provide responses to adverse effects of protectionism, but because it will act to maintain the credibility of the multilateral trade system in the minds of the general public. In Hansenne's view, the ILO's commitment to the multilateral trade system helps to keep globalization on track and obstruct tendencies to retreat into protectionism. Helping to keep globalization on track does not involve the ILO seeking "to achieve uniformity in the level of social protection in order to ensure a proper international competition. Rather the idea is simply to place social progress into a relationship with the economic progress expected from the liberalization of trade and globalization."[10]

There is ambiguity writ large in the notion of "relationship" in the previous quotation. Hansenne clearly did not envisage a joint process between the ILO and, for example, the WTO. His, at least in relation to the WTO, was not the later view of Somavia in which collaboration with international agencies figured large. Rather, Hansenne imagined a parallel process, based on globalization, in which the ILO promoted the social dimension of globalization, and the WTO the trade dimension, and in which any idea of a common global social protection framework played little or no part. He made this clear in other ways. He argued that the trade–labor standards discussion had been "a false debate because it was based on the implicit premise that trade liberalization should be subject to a certain level of standardization with regard to social protection—but that this was in no way realistic or in line with ILO principles." He made a strong case for "relativism," that is, different levels of social protection appropriate to different levels of development. Moreover, he argued, those differences are the source of economic advantage on which future social development is dependent. Hence, "[t]he main issue is not ... to impose standard regulations from the outside. What matters is that each Member should try to act in accordance with its possibilities, in consultation with its social partners, and that these efforts can be objectively demonstrated at the international level."

The phrase "must try to act" is telling, for it signals avoidance of mechanisms involving enforced compliance. The link between the declaration, and its refocusing of ILO priorities, and the trade–labor standards debate was thus established. In its own sphere of influence (social protection, or the social dimensions of globalization, or the social pillar of the global architecture) the ILO should seek to encourage and promote areas of fundamental rights alongside other positive outcomes from globalization. In this role, there was no place for the ILO to support the Social Clause in the WTO process. Linkage was not on the ILO's agenda, nor, by the later 1990s, was collaboration with the WTO (despite that possibility being raised in WTO ministerials). With the adoption of the declaration in 1998, the trade–labor standards linkage no longer figured prominently in ILO discussions and documents.

Under Somavia, circumstances changed. The World Commission on the Social Dimensions of Globalisation report in 2004 highlighted the need for greater dialogue across international agencies. As a result, the ILO introduced a Policy Coherence Initiative (PCI), beginning with an initiative on "Growth, Investment and Employment" with the Bretton Woods institutions and other multilateral agencies. The PCI is one of a range of measures to promote agency collaboration, including the UN's Millennium Development Goals, the ILO/United Nations Development Programme (UNDP) Memorandum of Understanding, and aspects of the ongoing UN reform process. By 2003, links between the ILO and the WTO were emerging as a direct effect of Somavia's commitment to institutional linkage, and the 2007 Joint ILO/WTO Report on Trade and Employment was a product of that linkage.

Distancing the Social Clause model

The Social Clause debate also raised internal concerns about the future of the ILO. Thus far, we have focused on the wider politics of the debate and how they were reflected in ILO discussions. Discussions in the ILO around the Social Clause also reflected the concerns from the director-general down about the impact on the ILO's status of a successful implementation of such a clause. The ILO's epistemic community became concerned that success would mean a diminution, even marginalization, of the ILO in its key area of standard-setting and monitoring. That concern was for the future of the ILO as an institution, and for the specialist roles within the institution. To understand this, we need to understand how the Social Clause might have operated.

The implementation of a Social Clause would most likely have been through mechanisms embodied in the procedures of the WTO. For example, two frequently canvassed options for including labor standards in the WTO system were amendments of either Article XX or Article XXIII of the GATT. Article XX, sometimes called the general exceptions article, allows a contracting party to restrict trade legitimately if, for example, it is necessary to protect life, or meet the requirements of law which are not inconsistent with the GATT, or relate to the conservation of exhaustible resources. It would be possible to include in Article XX wording relating to core labor standards. A second option might be to amend Article XXIII, which allows a contracting party to take action against another party if, because of actions by the other party which fail to meet obligations under the GATT, benefits that should have been gained have been lost or reduced (nullified or impaired). Further amendments to the GATT might be required to allow effective enforcement of labor standards in the case of both options. Effective enforcement would probably be under the auspices of the established dispute settlement mechanism.

For the ILO, what then would be its role? In the many versions of the Social Clause, the ILO's major role would be to provide the core standards. Thereafter, the responsibility for enforcement would lie solely with the WTO. Not only would the guardianship of core labor have passed to another international institution, but also, in contrast to the ILO's main weapon, moral suasion, the WTO would have a significantly stronger enforcement mechanism. The social partners and the staff in the ILO feared that this might constitute a serious blow to the status and reach of the ILO, for it might no longer be the effective global guardian of labor standards. Ways of inserting the ILO in the process were considered, such as requiring an ILO panel to be involved in the assessment of any alleged breach of core labor standards before reference to the WTO disputes process, but it is probable that, had the Social Clause been enacted, the WTO would have wanted to manage its own house.

There were, therefore, three factors underpinning Hansenne's adoption of a parallel and distant path to that of the WTO on trade and labor standards, The first was the impasse within the WTO; the second was the impasse within the ILO; the third, often overlooked, was a defensive posture adopted by some in the ILO as it sought to protect its own status and future.[11]

The Social Clause, the ILO and enforcement

The Social Clause debate highlights a long-standing issue for the ILO. The prevailing rhetoric surrounding labor standards is positive. Countries usually wish to be seen to have reasonable standards in place, employers likewise. Unions, of course, are firmly in favor of good labor standards. Thus, labor standards can lend themselves to platitudinal comment. When, however, it comes to enforcement, most governments and employers are equally certain that the traditional approach of the ILO (moral suasion, coupled with pressure to enact conventions in domestic law) is the appropriate way to deliver good labor standards. Nowhere is this more striking than in the case of the United States. A strong proponent of the Social Clause in the WTO process, the United States has, as we noted in Chapter 1, ratified only two of the core ILO conventions. It was also a strong supporter of the promotion and encouragement approach proposed by Hansenne and adopted in the 1998 declaration.

As discussed in Chapter 2, the ILO's traditional enforcement tools involve monitoring the application of conventions.[12] Monitoring and evaluation are increasingly onerous, with over 7,000 ratifications now in place, and with the reporting requirements association with the follow-up to the 1998 declaration adding to the burden. Article 22 of the ILO constitution demands of member states regular reports on the conventions ratified. The constitution also allows countries to be asked why conventions have not been ratified (Article 19). This information is analyzed annually within the ILO.[13] The International Labour Conference also has a watchdog role over the performance of conventions in member states.[14] Article 24 allows any social partner to make a complaint about a member state thought to be in breach of its commitments vis-à-vis a convention. The ILO has the power to investigate such breaches (via a commission of enquiry under Article 26), including the power to send a formal investigation team into the accused member state (albeit only with the consent of the government concerned). If, as in 2000 in the case of Burma's use of forced labor, an enquiry under Article 26 shows a country to be breach of conventions, Article 33 provides that

> [i]n the event of any Member failing to carry out within the time specified the recommendations, if any, contained in the report of the Commission of Inquiry, or in the decision of the International

Court of Justice, as the case may be, the Governing Body may recommend to the Conference such action as it may deem wise and expedient to secure compliance therewith.

The Burmese case was the first invocation of Article 33 in the ILO's history. In response, as the ILO web page puts it, "the Governing Body asked the International Labor Conference to take measures to lead Myanmar to end the use of forced labor." In other words, "naming and shaming" the Burmese government was accompanied by a strategy, in line with the 1998 declaration, to encourage Burma to end the use of forced labor.

Hansenne, arguing that this is consistent with the established ILO tradition, made a strong plea for the ILO to avoid attempts to impose standards from outside, but rather to come alongside countries and work within the possibilities for progress that might exist (see above).[15] The example of China comes to mind in this regard. "Telling" China what to do about labor standards is unlikely to bring positive results. Encouraging China to reform its labor standards (as it did, for example, in early 2008) might well be a more effective approach. Moreover, providing technical support to help the Chinese government in the decision about how to reform its labor relations system, and then implement changes, might embed a relationship with the ILO.

It would be wrong to underestimate the impact of the moral suasion and "naming and shaming" approach on countries failing to implement reasonable labor standards. It is always possible to dismiss ILO censure as irrelevant, uninformed, or given by an anachronistic institution of no importance. Yet, no government wishes to be held up to international criticism in relation to its labor standards.[16] It causes ministerial embarrassment and the possibility of adverse international media comment. In a globally integrated world, it may also have an impact on decisions around the location of FDI as companies reflect on an association with, in respect of its labor standards, a pariah country. Yet, in the absence of a strong, rules-based enforcement option (such as the WTO's dispute settlement procedure), the ILO has settled for a gradualist approach in which pressure and encouragement, combined with technical assistance, have sought to establish labor standards in member states. The promotion and encouragement approach of the declaration is consistent with this long-established gradualism.

Conclusion: where to after the Social Clause?

Our story of the Social Clause reveals both the highly contentious nature of the debate and the politically nuanced way in which the ILO has responded. As late as the Cancun ministerial in 2003, calls for such a clause to be attached to multilateral trade agreements were still part of official WTO deliberations. The continued rejection of this call underlined the gradual, and ultimately terminal, decline in political support for a WTO-patrolled social clause.[17] Great energy and commitment had been put into the Social Clause debate, and the failure to gain a linkage between labor standards and trade agreements might have been a major blow to the reputation and future of the ILO. Steering the ILO through this debate and emerging more relevant to the system of global governance was one of the defining features of Hansenne's tenure as the director-general of the ILO. It was also a key issue for his successor, Juan Somavia, who has courted deeper engagement with the International Monetary Fund and the World Bank while introducing a seemingly all-encompassing emphasis on globalization and Decent Work. Somavia's approach reflects the traditional ILO approach to difficulties. If the Social Clause was impossible to achieve, there must be other ways for the ILO to establish a greater global role and also become more engaged with the major international financial institutions. Hansenne's reform of the ILO provided a platform for Somavia to develop an alternative positioning for the ILO. It is to an examination of Somavia's ILO that we turn next.

6 Decent Work, Fair Globalisation, and strategic planning
Somavia's ILO

In previous chapters, we have shown how the leadership of Director-General Michel Hansenne refocused the ILO's activities in response to the challenge of globalization. The 1998 Declaration on Fundamental Principles and Rights at Work was the reference point for this refocusing. The adoption of the declaration was Hansenne's swansong. The Chilean, Juan Somavia, was elected to serve as director-general in 1998, his term beginning in early 1999. He had already played an important role as chair of the Preparatory Committee for the Copenhagen World Summit. It was in the Copenhagen summit that core labor standards were clearly identified. To quote the final report of the summit, governments should be:

> Safeguarding and promoting respect for basic workers' rights, including the prohibition of forced labor and child labor, freedom of association and the right to organize and bargain collectively, equal remuneration for men and women for work of equal value, and non-discrimination in employment, fully implementing the conventions of the International Labour Organisation (ILO) in the case of States parties to those conventions, and taking into account the principles embodied in those conventions in the case of those countries that are not States parties to thus achieve truly sustained economic growth and sustainable development;
> … Strongly considering ratification and full implementation of ILO conventions in these areas, as well as those relating to the employment rights of minors, women, youth, persons with disabilities and indigenous people;
> … Using existing international labor standards to guide the formulation of national labor legislation and policies; … Promoting the role of ILO, particularly as regards improving the *level of employment and the quality of work*.[1]

It is from this background that Somavia assumed the mantle of Albert Thomas. He moved the ILO forward on the track begun at the Copenhagen summit, and implemented by his predecessor, whilst also making his own mark on the process. That mark owes much to the agenda laid out in Copenhagen. The *A Fair Globalisation* report was produced at his instigation, and other work was carried out in the ILO by a Working Party on the Social Dimensions of Globalisation.[2] In turn, this resulted in the seminal 2008 Declaration on Social Justice for a Fair Globalisation. Much of this activity was in line with the conclusions drawn in Copenhagen. Somavia's openness to ILO co-operation with other international agencies reflected a theme in the Copenhagen final report as does his Decent Work agenda, which also drew on ILO traditions. Somavia also strove to improve the accountability of the ILO in terms of its strategic direction and the measurement and reporting to outcomes against strategic goals. The focus of this chapter will be on the Decent Work agenda, the principal initiative of his period in office, the follow-up to activities around the *A Fair Globalisation* report, and his strategic planning approach.

Decent Work: Somavia's imprint on the ILO

In a report to the International Labour Conference in 1999, Somavia described the ILO as:

> the global reference point for knowledge on employment and labour issues; the centre for normative action in the world of work; a platform for international debate and negotiation on social policy; and a source of services for advocacy, information and policy formulation ... the ILO must once again display its historic capacity for adaptation, renewal and change.[3]

That capacity required, argued Somavia, the setting of priorities and meant that "focus, excellence and effectiveness must guide the management culture of the house." Subsequently, he also recognized that the 1998 declaration provided the "universal floor," embodied in the fundamental principles and rights expressed in the core conventions.

Having established the status of the ILO, the need for priorities and for excellence, Somavia made a remarkable leap in reducing the vision and role of the ILO to one pithy statement: "The primary goal of the ILO today is to promote opportunities for women and men to obtain decent and productive work, in conditions of freedom, equity, security and human dignity." From this emerged the organizing principle for the ILO in the post-1999 period (Decent Work) and its role as epicenter of the four strategic objectives of the ILO.

The concept of Decent Work was much elaborated after Somavia introduced it in 1999.[4] Much of the discussion sought to position Decent Work as, simultaneously, a reflection of ILO traditions and a modernization to meet a new and different world. A key point was that the traditional ILO approach of standard-setting was too much driven by developed world country agendas. Even in its initial "development phase" in the 1960s to 1980s, when development issues were explicitly given a central role in ILO thinking, that traditional ILO approach was still powerful, and unbalancing in its effects. Decent Work, as a unity of the four strategic objectives, was able to deal with diversity in country experience more effectively, and therefore able to position the ILO in more balanced fashion across the needs of its constituents. Decent Work was also understood as universal. All people should enjoy decent work conditions and experience. The four strategic objectives encompass, in their unity, the key facets of Decent Work. Relativism will apply. Decent Work in Bangladesh may be configured differently from Decent Work in Sweden, and will be different again in Liberia, but it will have a clear meaning in each context. Moreover, each will be a site in which particular projects, capacity building and technical assistance can be implemented (see Figure 6.1).

The four strategic objectives define the breadth of ILO involvement proposed by the Decent Work paradigm. Rights at work respond to the traditional standard-setting activities of the ILO. Decent employment and income captures the ILO's long-standing commitment to macroeconomic policy, which promotes full employment and rewarding work opportunities. The emphasis on social protection reflects the ILO's engagement with social policy in parallel with macroeconomic policy. Social dialogue is simultaneously at the heart of the ILO process and, also, a commitment to strong democratic principles and institutions in and beyond work.

Somavia, in a more developed statement of the potential of Decent Work, argued that the agenda was challenging, but had to be achieved, for the ILO as an institution and for the world.[5] He charted the array of deficits in each of the strategic objectives and saw in those deficits the potential for an effective ILO work plan. He returned to a key theme in his thinking—the preparedness of the ILO to deliver that work plan. As he put it:

> it has traditionally been difficult to develop a capacity for integrated thinking, co-operation among programmes and a sense of teamwork

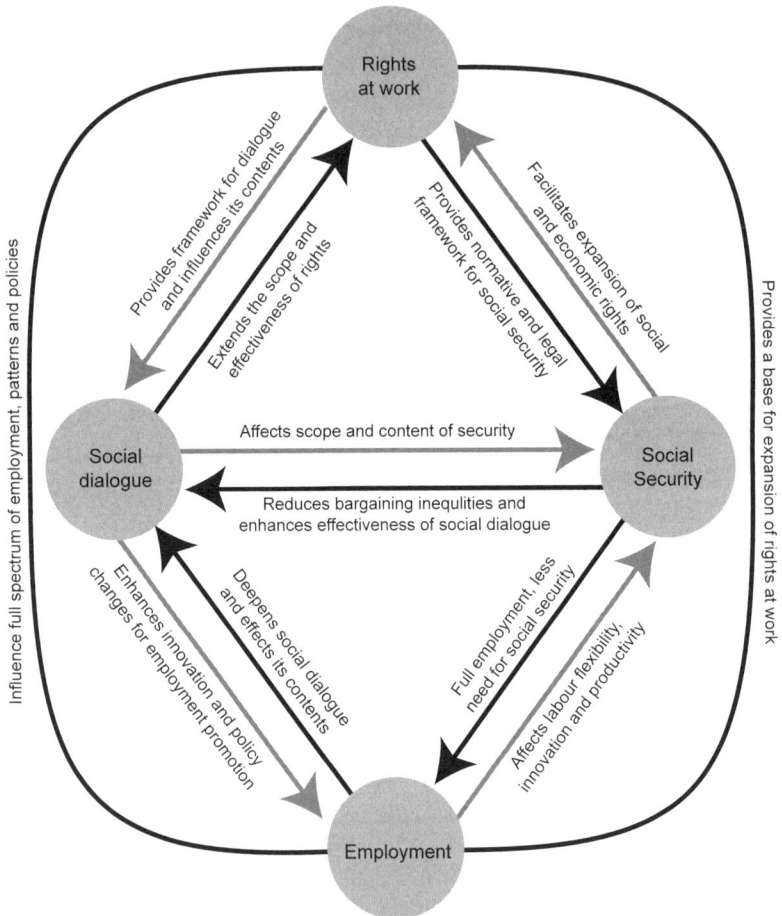

Figure 6.1 Relationships between the strategic objectives
Source: Ghai, 2006, p. 23

within the Office. This has also been true of our constituents, who have tended to pick and choose their preferences from the ILO menu. This has regularly come to the fore in the programme and budget debates ... I honestly believe that a fragmented ILO has no future. We need to change old habits.[6]

One senses frustration in Somavia about the internal performance of the ILO and, also about the level and quality of commitment of the social partners to a strong and effective ILO. His is, publicly, a more striking critique of the ILO than that of Hansenne, yet they share much in common. The structure of the ILO, the configuration and performance of staff and programs, the quality of thinking and representativity of the social partners, and the quality of strategic thinking uniting the whole are central to the assessments made by both.

The implementation of Decent Work was entrusted in the first instance to the Decent Work Pilot Programme (DWPP) which oversaw pilot interventions in eight countries seeking to integrate Decent Work into national policy-making by, in particular, strengthening capacity building.[7] Subsequently, a variety of related programs were introduced, including, in 2002, pilot projects looking to integrate Decent Work into poverty reduction strategies (the Poverty Reduction Strategy Papers process—PRSP).[8] Other, parallel initiatives were commenced with Brazil, Argentina and some Asian region countries. In 2005, the idea of Decent Work Country Programmes was launched, involving national programs with high levels of integration of Decent Work priorities.

Awad's review of the DWPP makes the point that, at inception, the Decent Work pilot projects had no experience to go on. First principles had to be developed, which promoted integrated interventions based on the four strategic objectives, met national needs and priorities, and mobilized the appropriate resources. Thus, in each pilot country, the social partners were actively engaged in the definition of the agenda to be followed. Inevitably, countries produced different plans. Moreover, those plans often cut across programs, with, for example, Decent Work becoming tied in to poverty reduction in many cases. For example, Ghana focused on Decent Work as a means to reduce poverty, in the context in which the Ghanaian Poverty Reduction Strategy was a national framework in which Decent Work could play a constructive role. The Philippines adopted decent and productive employment within its national development plan priorities, and tied that goal into its poverty reduction strategy. In a quite different context, the pilot study in Denmark showed how Decent Work strategies permit structural adjustment in developed economies to go forward without the undermining of social provision, ongoing job protections and high wages.

Awad's assessment of the DWPP was generally positive. The programs, she argued, helped to identify and integrate policy priorities for the participating countries. Policy coherence was an important positive outcome. The advantages of national social dialogue as a means of embedding policy priorities were apparent, as was the effect of the pilot projects in linking domestic priorities with those emerging in the global economy. Equally, the projects helped to integrate national priorities with local initiatives within the pilot countries. Effective monitoring and evaluation were highlighted as an important condition for success. Finally, the role of technical assistance and capacity building was central to success, and showed the need to have available the appropriate training and tools in support of the Decent Work agenda.[9]

The ILO has undertaken a variety of approaches to the Decent Work agenda since its introduction in 2000. For example, Buckley provides an assessment of the impact of the Decent Work agenda in the PRSP program in Ethiopia.[10] His conclusion is that there are both technical and principled dimensions to the successful use of Decent Work in poverty reduction programs. Technically, competent databases on domestic labor markets are essential for understanding and measuring the impact of Decent Work on poverty reduction. In their absence, the ability of Decent Work initiatives to strengthen analysis and support implementation will be undermined. Equally important, the integration of the ILO's four strategic objectives in the Decent Work agenda emphasizes the need for similar integration of policies domestically if the "entitlements deficit" which for the poor blocks their access to many advantages, including Decent Work, is to be overcome. Buckley finds in the notion of Decent Work "a cross-cutting, holistic concept which should have an impact greater than the sum of its four constituent parts (rights at work, employment, social protection and social dialogue)."

By the time the 2006/7 ILO budget was announced, Decent Work Country Programmes (DWCP) were to be its main delivery vehicles.[11] In line with the rationalization of programs and budgets discussed below, a DWCP was to be the operational framework for ILO activities in any country. The elements determining a DWCP were a clear problem analysis, leading to the identification of clear priorities which reflected national priorities, those of the social partners and other agencies operating in the country. Technical assistance needs were also identified at this stage. Short- (2 year) and medium-term (4–6 year) goals were set, associated with an implementation plan that defined goals and their evaluation. Monitoring and evaluation permitted adjustment of, and a check on, the impact of the program. At the heart of each country program were the ILO's four strategic objectives, technical assistance, monitoring and evaluation. A first-time reader of the DWCP material from the ILO would understand the ILO's intervention strategy as a broad approach to labor and social issues in a given country. Whilst rights at work remained one of the four strategic objectives underpinning Decent Work, that reader would have had to search to discover the remnants of the traditional ILO focus on standard-setting. The DWCP, as the primary delivery vehicle for the ILO budget, indicated clearly how far the reform process begun in 1994 had taken the

ILO. By 2008, DWCPs were in place in 31 member states, with another 53 in preparation.

To be fair, the annual director-general's report maintained an express link with the past.[12] The first strategic objective to be reported was that covering the promotion and realization of standards and fundamental principles and rights at work. However, the reporting framework places that objective, not only in the context of the remaining three objectives, but also of other delivery methods, such as "mainstreamed strategies" on globalization, poverty, gender equality, social dialogue and tripartism and the "[g]reater influence of international labor standards in development." Other initiatives were also reported. It was difficult not to see the ILO's standard-setting role as an important, but not pre-eminent, aspect of its work plan. The work on conventions and recommendations went ahead within the ILO, but its presence and status was mediated by its status within the Strategic Policy Framework.

The status of Decent Work in ILO strategy brings to life the debates rehearsed in Chapter 4 around the 1998 declaration. Langille's critique of Alston included pragmatic questions about the impact of the declaration and the shift to core rights. Will Decent Work-related programs bring about real improvement in people's lives? Are they a good thing? Do they stand the ILO in good stead for the future? Empirically, there is some evidence that the programs are successful. They are certainly growing in number and extent. We can also reflect on the likely advantages of an integrated, country-based program in which ILO activities are associated closely with national policy setting and the activities of other international agencies. Improved monitoring and evaluation designed to upgrade performance may well conserve scarce resources. There is also a strong continuity between the purpose of the 1998 declaration and the development of the Decent Work agenda. The post-1994 change process is purposely consolidated in Decent Work.

Fair Globalization

In June, 2008, the International Labour Conference adopted the Declaration on Social Justice for a Fair Globalization.[13] This was a direct effect of the follow-up undertaken after the *Fair Globalisation* report, and of the activities of the Working Party on the Social Dimensions of Globalization.[14] It also draws significantly on other initiatives, including the Copenhagen Social Summit. Its constitutional status within the ILO is as one of three supreme statements of ILO principles and values. The other two are the Declaration of Philadelphia (1944) and the Declaration on Fundamental Principles and Rights at Work (1998).

The 2008 declaration positioned the ILO as the pretender to the pre-eminent role in the creation of global social justice and a fair globalization. It also positioned the Decent Work agenda as the key delivery mechanism to achieve those ends. It located Decent Work in the four strategic objectives of the ILO (employment, social protection, social dialogue and international labor standards) and as central to the design and implementation of the Strategic Policy Framework (2010–15). A key argument made by Somavia was that the four objectives are indivisible, that is, each is vital for the achievement of the others. The ILO is the only international institution commanding the principles and values, the track record and the technical capacities able to achieve these objectives. The implementation of the 2008 declaration was in line with the implementation of the 1998 declaration. The follow-up process envisaged the ILO putting in place resources and capacities able to support members as they implemented the 2008 declaration's principles. Support for member states would be in terms of improved and focused technical assistance, good research provision and effective evaluation of the 2008 declaration by the International Labour Conference.

The 2008 declaration also signals the moving-on of the ILO from the politics of the 1998 declaration. The 1998 declaration was a repositioning or refocusing exercise, allowing the ILO to identify fundamental areas of action in a process of prioritization. It also reaffirmed strongly the promotion and encouragement model, whilst distancing the ILO to some extent from a traditional standard-setting focus. The two processes (prioritization and distancing) provided the "space" in which, from 1999, the four strategic objectives could be defined, and for the broader mandate for social justice to be assumed. Decent Work provides the framework for meeting that mandate.

The ILO: strategy and performance

Somavia came to office with a clear view that the performance of the ILO might be improved. In Chapter 3, we indicated his concerns about the inward-looking nature of the ILO. He saw the ILO as "inward looking, preoccupied with procedure, relatively slow in response, and having a style of expression that deters all but the most enthusiastic from discovering our ideas."[15] He also thought it poorly focused in terms of outputs and outcomes. Hence, immediately upon taking up his position, he set in train a change process involving strong tripartite consensus around ILO priorities, budget reallocations and a work program to meet those priorities, and new management structures and program activities.[16] For the initial period (2002–5), tripartite consensus was reached around the four strategic objectives, which were to:

- promote and realize standards and fundamental principles and rights at work;
- create greater opportunities for women and men to secure decent employment and income;
- enhance the coverage and effectiveness of social protection for all; and
- strengthen tripartism and social dialogue.

Each was refined by subsets of operational objectives and a statement of ILO responses to those objectives. Subsequent reporting was provided in terms of those objectives. The same strategic objectives were included in the Strategic Policy Framework (SPF) for 2010–15, which emphasized an explicitly outcomes-based approach to ILO activities.[17] The SPF set out the objectives for the ILO in a measurable, results-based manner. Its design sought to be both stable and flexible, able to show changing performance over time, yet also allowing for adaptation in the work program. The director-general's annual reports were also structured in terms of strategic objectives, outputs and outcomes, and measurement of targets reached (or not). Integration and cross-cutting themes were important, with cross-cutting activities including emphases on policy integration, gender equality, research and training, and external relations and partnerships.

Somavia's management reforms were significant and inevitably challenged many ILO staff members. Thirty-nine major programs were reorganized into the four strategic objectives in a substantial budget and program realignment. A new senior management team was installed. The technical sectors within the ILO were restructured internally. Operational objectives were reviewed and revised and cost-benefit measures and performance measurement were introduced. Monitoring, evaluation and reporting were revised and made more responsive to budget process requirements. Eight international focus programs (InFocus) linked to the strategic objectives were identified. Building on elements in the present work of the Office, they cut across existing departmental boundaries to concentrate a critical mass of research and technical co-operation in areas such as strengthening social dialogue, the elimination of child labor, and crisis response and reconstruction.

The social partners broadly supported these reforms. In many ways, they saw them as a necessary complement to the refocusing of the ILO in the 1990s. Some staff members were also comfortable with change in the organization. For them, modernization of the ILO was overdue, and a focus on performance was welcome. There is a counterview, put most eloquently and forcefully by Standing.[18] In that counterview, leadership in the ILO was weakened after 1999 by the appointment to senior and line management positions of "faction" members, that is, employers and trade unionists. Roles were therefore "muddied" as appointees struggled to match their technical and "political" responsibilities. Then, the transition to a new director-general did little or nothing to address the fundamental question of representativity. The union and employer organizations within the ILO, argues Standing, represent at best a small part of their potential global constituency. Moreover, they have a stranglehold over their own fiefdoms within the ILO and are unlikely to want to give up that power. There is no willingness to think and act more widely about the contemporary structure of work and what that might mean in terms of representation in the ILO. The abolition of the Industrial Relations Department in 1999, suggests Standing, seriously reduced the focus on labor standards, allowing the much vaguer and "vacuous" notion of social dialogue to prevail. Budgets for the traditional standards work were squeezed by other expenditures (with Standing estimating, for example, that work on the *Fair Globalisation* report may have cost up to US$20 million). Standard-setting has also been undermined by increased numbers of staff with no experience of standards and the ILO process (including the highest levels of leadership). The new budget model introduced a tendency to "short-termism," for it runs on a two-year cycle.

This is a strong attack on structure of the ILO post-1999, and, it must be said, very much directed at the strategic vision of successive directors-general, and particularly at the changes brought in by Director-General Somavia. It is also simply one aspect of a far broader attack on the current ILO by Standing, who argues that the flawed strategic direction chosen by the ILO after 1994, and particularly after 1999, has compounded problems already in place at the time of Hansenne's election. We return to this attack in Chapter 8. For now, we might reflect on the size of the challenge facing Somavia when he began his reorganization of the ILO.

The ILO is a large, complex, ponderous international "political" bureaucracy, multi-sited, highly formal, hierarchical, and multicultural. Its staff is diverse, varying from essentially political appointments to highly skilled and highly specialized technical staff, many with international reputations in their fields of expertise. There is, particularly in the specialist groups, a strong ethos of guardianship of their respective areas of responsibility and of ILO traditions. Quality outputs matter, but so does the responsibility of meeting the requirements of a diverse audience, especially amongst the social partners. Much as is the case with a national civil service, which develops its mechanisms and manner of expression to match its advisory role to government, so the specialist "officials" of the ILO measure their outputs. Its epistemic community may well have contributed to the successful survival of the ILO, but it is also often defensive and, as Somavia put it, inward-looking, regulation-focused and unapproachable. As one thwarted senior staff member loyal to the post-1994 change process put it in the early 2000s: "Achieving change here is very difficult ... there is obstruction all the way ... organizational politics here are poisonous."[19]

This context is important when we consider the scope of change envisaged by Hansenne and Somavia. Putting to one side the rights and wrongs of the ILO's refocusing post-1994, consensus for that refocusing was achieved amongst the social partners and the directors-general received a mandate for change. They were faced with a major external challenge as they repositioned the ILO in the new global order, but the external challenge was matched by an equally difficult internal challenge, for some ILO staffers were angered by what they saw as a misdirection of the ILO and, therefore, a potential threat to the ILO's future. The fact that the repositioning caused internal reorganization of the ILO, which shifted boundaries, changed responsibilities and had significant effects on the career prospects of many staff members, should not be forgotten. We should take care when judging the need for, and impact of, Somavia's organizational and managerial reforms, and when we consider the competing interpretations of those reforms, for there are many interests in play.

The Somavia legacy

Somavia is the first director-general in the ILO's history from a developing country. He had little previous history with the ILO before he was elected. He is not a labor specialist but, rather, an international diplomat with a strong interest in development and social justice. He had no grounding in the pre-1994 period, that period which Langille sees as romanticized by those with a narrow labor law perspective on the ILO.[20] The links between his own thinking and the changes introduced by Hansenne were explicitly recognized in the latter's references to the outcome of the Copenhagen Social Summit, a summit in which Somavia had played a leading role. We must assume that Somavia's election reflected broad comfort with his track record and policy preferences. In the context of the post-1994 changes, Somavia had an unequivocal mandate to continue the reform process. Any surprise that he did would be contrary. A performance review might well agree that he had operated in the manner expected at the time of appointment and probably met his key performance indicators. All three social partners issued strongly worded statements of support for him and his programs when he was re-elected in 2003. He was, undoubtedly, seen as an inappropriate appointment or threat by some ILO staff.[21] Following his appointment, factional commentary emerged within the organization around his suitability for the job, his senior staff appointments and, inevitably the changes in priority and management that he introduced. This is not surprising, nor is the concern expressed by some staff members about the "cult of the individual" sometimes attributed to Somavia. Visible leadership often attracts such commentaries, and the leader of a complex and highly political organization such as the ILO will usually have something of an ego.

Weighing up Somavia's term in office, it is fair to conclude that his was an appointment well-fitted to the task bequeathed to him by Hansenne. Somavia has extended the change process strategically and organizationally, and with success, and has undoubtedly placed the ILO more firmly in the public gaze and in the deliberations of other international agencies.

Conclusion

From the ILO's perspective, Somavia reinforced the change process begun by Hansenne. Somavia's period in office has confirmed the heading on which the ILO is set. After more than 20 years of concerted change, the ILO is a different organization today from that which Hansenne took over in the 1980s. The ILO will be defined in the future by its mission to establish labor standards and social justice as a core component of global governance. That mission will emphasize collaboration between international organizations in which the ILO will seek to be a leading player. Collaboration benefits from a capacity to change to meet new circumstances, and we can, therefore, expect the ILO to experience further shifts in structure and strategic focus. In turn, the debate within and around the ILO about its principles and purpose will be hard-fought. The contemporary structure of that debate is addressed in Chapter 8.

7 The ILO at work in the 2007 global economic crisis

In 2007, the global economy began its plunge into crisis. Explanations for the crisis vary, but most commentators agree that it began as a financial crisis in the United States. According to the OECD, after 2004, there was an "explosion" of residential mortgage-backed securities, impelled by four factors: ready access to zero equity mortgages for low-income families; extra prudential requirements placed on Fannie Mae and Freddie Mac, allowing private banks to invade their market territory; the acceleration of off-balance-sheet activities by banks following the Basel II accords; less stringent oversight of banks allowing them to increase their lending.[1] The effect was to allow a massive growth in low-quality mortgages to the tune of US$1.3 trillion. Investment banks, using a dynamic business model focusing on improved profits and rapid share price growth, were particularly active in securitization, and significantly underestimated the risks involved in this expansionary dynamic. The logic of the business model drew banks into increasingly poor decisions as they sought to maintain fee streams from the securitization of low quality mortgages. By mid-2007, when BNP Paribas announced the suspension of three of its funds with investments in US mortgage securities, the prospect of major global financial difficulty became real. When, subsequently, in the United States, then internationally, liquidity dried up, the model collapsed as did many major financial institutions, first in the United States, then beyond. Other developed economies suffered similar lending and liquidity problems. The 2008 "sub-prime" crisis reverberated around the world as global liquidity fell and economies began to suffer serious negative impacts. Within months, fears grew that the biggest economic crisis since the inter-war years was about to plunge the global economy into depression.

By late 2009, the World Bank was describing the crisis as the severest credit crunch and depression to face the world since the Great

Depression.[2] The global economy "came to a halt" in the second half of 2008, with global trade predicted to fall in 2009 for the first time since 1982. Developed world GDP was predicted to fall by 3.8 percent in 2009, against 0.9 percent growth in 2008, and developing country GDP was expected to fall by 1.6 percent in 2009, against a 6.1 percent growth in 2008. In response, governments poured massive support into their economies in order to bolster liquidity (and, hence, investment, companies, jobs and trade) and the battered financial sector.

The adverse employment consequences of the crisis exhibited the ILO at its technical best. It undertook a detailed study of the employment consequences of the crisis. The work was completed as an effect of a call made by G20 leaders at their April 2009 London Summit on Growth, Stability and Jobs. At that summit, the G20 leaders adopted a Global Plan for Recovery and Reform and called on the ILO to assess labor market measures taken in response to the crisis, and other measures that might be taken in the future. The consequent report, from which the following data are drawn, was presented by Director-General Somavia at the Pittsburgh summit of G20 leaders in September 2009.[3] We will return to the politics of engagement between the ILO and the G20 shortly. We focus here on the employment impacts of the crisis.

The data presented by the ILO in its report reflect the severity of the crisis. For example, taking the G20 economies, by March 2009, unemployment was, on average, 1.5 percent higher than a year previously (8.5 percent). Across the 54 countries surveyed, the total of unemployed was 23.6 percent higher over the same period (March 2008–March 2009). Unemployment increased for the June 2008–June 2009 year by 69 percent in the United States, 44 percent in Canada, 42 percent in Australia, and 26 percent in Korea. In Russia, the increase was 83 percent in the June year, 55 percent in the April year for Turkey, and 38 percent in the March year for the United Kingdom.

The employment impacts of crisis were different for different sectors of the labor market. Women had, in the first phase of the crisis (2008–9) seen a lower increase in unemployment, but on an unemployment base that was higher than that of men at the start of the crisis. The ILO predicted that, as the crisis continued, the rate of unemployment increase for women would catch up with that of men. Youth unemployment jumped also as an effect of the crisis, for example rising in the European Union from 15.4 percent to 19.7 percent between July 2008 and June 2009. Indicative data were provided to support the case that unemployment is complemented by a strong "discouragement" effect.

The ILO report also investigated the GDP effects of the crisis. The evidence showed that the relationship between GDP shifts and unemployment was country-specific. In some countries (for example, Spain and the United Kingdom), GDP decline had been sharp (more than 4 percent in the 2008–9 year), as had the increase in unemployment (more than 1.6 percent). In others (Germany, Italy, Japan and Mexico, for example), sharp GDP decline was accompanied by moderate unemployment growth (less that 1.3 percent). A third group (for example, Australia, Canada and the United States) displayed moderate GDP decline (less than 3 percent) yet sharp unemployment increase. Yet others (Brazil, Indonesia) were moderate in both GDP and unemployment decline. GDP decline also raised the issue of the impact of the crisis on poverty levels. In general, the ILO report argued that declining GDP growth was likely to reduce the rate of decline in poverty, whilst negative GDP growth would increase poverty levels. United Nations data suggested that the effects of the crisis might be to increase numbers in poverty by between 73 and 103 million, compared with a no-crisis scenario. The growth in the incidence of poverty was particularly strong in developing countries, which were also facing declining remittances, declining FDI and declining export opportunities. These economies also faced increased unemployment, but, equally important, did so in the context of, to use the ILO's term, "the already bloated informal economy."

The ILO report also looked at the labor market and social welfare responses across the surveyed countries. On the one hand, it was difficult to talk about one without reference to the other; on the other, the broader role of the ILO established from the inter-war years onwards required the ILO to move beyond labor market issues to broader social welfare consequences and responses. Countries were shown to have implemented programs to create and/or retain employment, by means of infrastructure spending, direct financial support to firms, and labor market adjustments to match better supply of, and demand for, labor. The ILO also looked in detail at the role of the public sector in the development of labor market responses to the crisis, and at the use of hiring subsidies and new skills and training measures. Finally, the report looked at innovations in social welfare provision designed to reduce adverse social impacts of the crisis.

The report reflected the ILO's long-established role. It was, first, a high-quality technical report based on carefully assessed empirical data. Second, it focused strongly on both labor market and social welfare dimensions of the crisis, illustrating the traditional extension of the ILO agenda beyond narrow employment and labor market issues. Third, there was little in the report that smacked of neo-liberalism. Whilst it was a reporting-back of the gathered data, the positioning of the

88 *The ILO and the 2007 global economic crisis*

analysis, especially around active labor market policies, asserted implicitly the usefulness of labor market and social welfare interventions to support recovery from the crisis. Fourth, its focus on particularly vulnerable sectors of the labor market, on developing countries, and on poverty measures, reflected traditional concerns in ILO analysis. Fifth, the report was practically orientated, it sought to be helpful for and relevant to practical policy-making. Finally, it was positioned to establish the ILO as the key international agency commenting on the broadly defined employment impacts of the crisis. That it was commissioned by the G20 in April 2009 reinforced that positioning. We now turn to the ILO link to the G20.

The ILO and the G20 in 2009

The G20 has become the "management committee" for the global economy.[4] Certainly, in September 2009, at its Pittsburgh meeting, the group described itself as "the premier forum for our international economic cooperation." Given its membership, that role extends in importance significantly beyond the immediate membership. This role has been substantially developed by the group's central role in generalizing responses to the current crisis. By late 2009 at its Pittsburgh meeting, the G20's response to the crisis was organized around a number of key themes.

First, the G20 emphasized the need for a new international economic architecture. This presumed the centrality of the G20 to global economic management. It also argued for greater voice in global decision-making for emerging markets and developing countries in the IMF and the World Bank, and a stronger and expanded Financial Stability Board and Global Forum. Second, the group called for strong, sustainable and balanced growth, including careful reflection and action by the developed economies on their regulatory regimes as an outcome of the sub-prime mortgage problem. Third, the group called for bold and co-ordinated action to move from crisis to recovery. The G20 was confident that the strong interventionist approaches adopted in member economies, and beyond, as an effect of G20 encouragement had been successful, for example, saving between 7 million and 11 million jobs between early 2008 and late 2009. Moreover, the group believed the decline in the rate of increase in unemployment followed from G20 policies as did the return to economic growth expected in 2010. Reductions in long-term lending risk were also argued to be a result of strong interventions by the G20, as were improving consumer confidence and exports. Fourth, the G20 emphasized the need for further work on global food security, building on the L'Aquila partnership of countries and international organizations founded in July 2009. Fifth, the Pittsburgh meeting emphasized the need for strong action on global energy and climate change challenges. Finally, the G20 committed its members to support for the most vulnerable, particularly in the developing world. Proposed actions included revised priorities for, and improved co-operation between, multilateral financial institutions, improved food security, improved access to clean energy and investment funds, and improved anti-corruption measures.

The power, and asserted pre-eminence, of the G20 in the global economy comes from its membership and reach. It constitutes about 85 percent of global GDP, 80 percent of world trade and 70 percent of the world's population. Crucially, it engages the United States and the European Union with Brazil, Russia, India and China (the "BRIC" countries). Its configuration and internal debates reflect the changing configuration of international economic power since the late 1970s. It is not surprising that it claimed at Pittsburgh a pre-eminent role in managing the global economy, for example, subsuming the Bretton Woods institutions under its general direction. It was, therefore, an important institution for the ILO in its post-1994 strategic positioning. If the ILO was to build and sustain its engagement with other multilateral agencies, establishing a strong link with the G20 was required. Hence, to be asked by the G20 at its April 2009 London summit to prepare a report for the September 2008 Pittsburgh meeting on the "socio-economic imbalances that existed already before the crisis and which contributed to it, expressed in rising income inequality, employment and social protection deficits and persisting poverty, and weakening labor institutions"[5] was an excellent opportunity for the ILO to participate at the "top table," a level of participation reinforced by the invitation offered to Somavia to present the report in person to the G20 leaders at Pittsburgh. This alone might be cited as strong evidence of successful repositioning of the ILO as an effect of shifts in focus and organization under Hansenne and Somavia.

It is possible to interpret this engagement with the G20 positively or negatively, depending on one's position on the post-1994 reconfiguration of the ILO. Understood positively, as noted above, participation in G20 deliberations established an important role for the ILO in crisis responses, and direct engagement with the key countries and leaders steering those responses. Taken in a negative light, one would still view the engagement with the G20 as a good example of the technical work which the ILO has always done well. However, the engagement with the G20 might be seen as superficial, transitory and, in the long run, potentially diverting the ILO from its proper role, that is, to protect labor standards. What is indisputable is that, for Somavia, the request to provide the technical report and to speak to the Pittsburgh summit was clear endorsement of the long-term role of the ILO in the area of labor markets, employment and social protection, and of the short-term focus on responses to the crisis undertaken in the ILO's preparation of the Global Jobs Pact, endorsed at the ILO's June 2009 International Labour Conference.[6] It is to the Global Jobs Pact that we now turn.

The ILO's Global Jobs Pact

The Global Jobs Pact was the major focus of ILO work in 2009, constituting its response to the challenges created by the global crisis. However, its origins are earlier, including in the Global Employment Agenda announced at the ILO's Governing Body in March 2008. In one of the director-general's reports to the June 2008 International Labour Conference, Somavia offered an initial understanding of the developing crisis, noting that, if other institutions were responsible for solutions for the financial dimensions of the crisis, it was also important for the ILO to take a position, based on the responsibilities established by the Declaration of Philadelphia.[7] In other words, Somavia gave a nod to the "division of labor" between international organizations, whilst also asserting firmly the right and responsibility of the ILO to become involved.

Somavia provided an analysis of the financial dimensions of the crisis, emphasizing its destabilizing impact on work. As money markets lost touch with reality, their behavior undermined productive behavior, and, hence, enterprise performance. The "real" economy suffered at the hands of the financial sector, which lost public and business confidence. Moreover, a finance-driven global economic model drove increased inequality globally and, also intensification of work in many countries, sectors and enterprises.

His analysis led him to the conclusion that a co-ordinated international approach to the crisis was needed, in which the ILO and, particularly, the Decent Work agenda, would play an important role. The context for this contribution was a policy rethink, under way as an effect of the crisis. The key elements of that rethink were government interventions on a large scale to stabilize the global system, coupled with increased social spending to tide affected people through the worst aspects of the crisis. As Somavia stated in his report to the International Labour Conference, "The ILO's Decent Work Agenda offers policy tools that have heightened relevance in a period of slowing growth."

How did Somavia explain this "heightened relevance"? He invoked a number of major themes associated with the Decent Work agenda, including its life-cycle approach, its focus on poverty and inequality reduction, its focus on the productive, "real" economy, its capacity to support effective social security and welfare interventions, and its engagement with skills and training. He also linked that relevance to the impact of ILO-driven interventions on "broad-based prosperity," emphasizing the impact of inclusive policy measures on the growth of a successful middle class in developing economies. There was a strong focus on coherence, between international institutions and their policy settings, especially in the UN system, and between countries in arrangements such as the G20. He also emphasized the importance of effective national co-ordination of institutions and policies.

He concluded his report with two strong themes. The first was a review of the extensive collaboration in place between the ILO and other multilateral agencies, simultaneously pointing out their past development, current strength and future potential. The second was a reprise of the Somavia message about the ILO's performance. It had to improve its structures and activities to meet the emerging challenges posed by the crisis. This would require, inter alia, improved resourcing, such that there was a resource base "commensurate with the ILO's role."

This, then, was Somavia's message in June 2008. It was a message of opportunity provided by the emerging crisis. The crisis provided an opportunity for the ILO to play a role in global responses to the crisis at the highest level. The ILO had the understanding and the tools, especially in the Decent Work agenda, to make a lasting contribution to renewed global economic stability. It was incumbent on the ILO to take this opportunity, but it had to ensure that the ILO was organizationally ready for the task ahead. It was a restatement of Somavia's established vision for the ILO, reframed in the context of the global crisis.

The International Labour Conference, meeting in June 2009, endorsed a Global Jobs Pact, which is the ILO initiative responding to the opportunity created by the crisis. The Pact seeks to promote an outcome from the crisis which minimizes social disruption and focuses on Decent Work outcomes in the recovery phase. With 300 million new jobs to be found by 2015 across the globe, the Pact is understood to be both necessary and a forceful response to the employment challenges facing the world. It is a portfolio of measures, addressing job retention and creation, more rapid re-entry into the labor market for those displaced, the impact of wage deflation, social protection (especially for the most vulnerable), and skill needs and development. It is located in the ILO, and its unique and important tripartite process and social dialogue framework, but also is designed to engage with the UN multilateral agencies and the Bretton Woods institutions. The Pact, as a package of measures, but also as a positioning measure for the ILO, was a key element in the ILO's engagement with the G20 later in 2009.

Somavia's address to the 98th International Labour Conference in 2009 laid out the strategic positioning of the Pact.[8] The rationale for the Pact rested in three factors: the Decent Work agenda, the ILO's position on globalization as manifest in the Declaration on Social Justice for a Fair Globalization, and the need to address the challenges posed by the crisis. Somavia painted a picture of a jobs and social protection crisis extending for up to eight years as the economic crisis unfolded. The scale of the crisis required a step-change in global responses to the human problems arising from the crisis. He also noted the threat to political stability posed by the employment effects of the crisis, echoing a traditional theme in the ILO's history.

The Pact was presented as the outcome of a range of initiatives and instructions, from the ILO's Governing Body meetings of November 2008 and March 2009, the outcomes of the G20 London jobs summit (discussed above), and the G8+6 Labor and Employment Ministers' Meeting in Rome, 2009. It was designed to be taken up on a multilateral, multi-agency basis, and was to be supported by an inter-agency joint initiative provided for by the United Nations Chief Executives' Board. The multi-agency approach also responded to funding requirements, as the Bretton Woods institutions were responsible for significant crisis-related expenditures (such as the World Bank's Vulnerability Financing Facility, and its associated Rapid Social Response Fund).

What would the Pact offer to global recovery? According to Somavia, it would support a more rapid solution of the crisis, whilst sustaining social stability. Its focus on Decent Work would also promote better quality employment outcomes than would otherwise be the case. Its key dimensions would include:

- Guaranteeing credit flows to business, especially small and medium-sized enterprises (a necessary precondition for employment retention and creation);
- Retention of viable jobs by means of a reduction in work hours and the targeted use of skill development strategies (to minimize unnecessary lay-offs and labor market disruption);
- Unemployment benefits targeted expressly to support job seekers;
- A strong focus on active labor market policies to reduce, first, the impact of unemployment and, second, to minimize social exclusion. Employment guarantee schemes were particularly highlighted;
- An equally strong focus on measures to support youth in the labor market;

- Investment in job-rich infrastructure projects;
- The development of "green" employment strategies to reinforce employment sustainability; and
- The extension of social protection to vulnerable groups currently without such protection.

The ILO and the crisis: assessing the Global Jobs Pact

The employment and social protection issues raised by the economic crisis were in many ways an ideal opportunity for the repositioned ILO to stake a claim at the "top table" of international agencies. It was an opportunity for the Somavia agenda to show itself to be relevant and effective on the global stage. A balanced assessment suggests that the ILO seized this opportunity successfully. It did so in a number of ways. First, it used its technical expertise to great effect in providing a technically competent, intervention-orientated assessment of the employment and social protection impacts of the crisis. Other international agencies, especially the G20, charged the ILO to carry out this work in explicit recognition of the ILO's role and expertise. Second, the work carried out by the ILO and the recommendations that followed, was more than a simple technical assessment of the crisis' employment impacts. The technical analysis was grounded in the ILO's strategic direction, that is, in the Decent Work agenda. Thus, the ILO began to frame the employment and social protection responses to the crisis within its own rhetoric and practices, in particular in terms of tripartism and social dialogue. Third, the involvement with the G20, including the invitation to the ILO director-general to participate in the meeting, was endorsement both of the technical expertise of the ILO and also its traditional message about labor market stability and political stability. One could argue that this endorsement bore out the wider "social protection" role assumed by the ILO in the Declaration of Philadelphia. Fourth, the ILO's independence was not challenged by this role. The request for action was made to the ILO as an independent body with a clear international mandate. If anything, it reinforced that independence, and may well have allayed, to some extent at least, fears in the ILO of a loss of status as a result of the post-1994 refocusing.

Conclusion

Director-General Somavia must have looked at the period after 2007 with mixed emotions. On the one hand, no-one could revel in the disruption and suffering caused by the economic global crisis. On the other, however, the crisis offered to the ILO an opportunity to engage at the highest level in the development of both economic and social policy responses to the recession. For the ILO, there is much in common with this crisis and that of the inter-war years. As we suggested in Chapter 1, one of the ways in which the ILO came to survive the demise of the League of Nations was by becoming a repository of knowledge and policy advice about responses to economic and social crisis. True to that tradition, the ILO has in the most recent crisis proved its continuing relevance, as a highly competent technical body, as a player at the top table with the main international agencies, and as an agency able to adjust to changing circumstances.

The ILO's work in response to the crisis has, in many ways, set the seal on the changes begun by Michel Hansenne, and continued by Juan Somavia. One could argue reasonably that as an effect of those changes the ILO is in a stronger position than at any time in its post-1945 history. Talk about the growing irrelevance of the ILO has been muted, Instead, its role, not only in terms of immediate responses to the crisis, but also in terms of its Decent Work agenda and ongoing co-operation with other international organizations, is viewed positively by the social partners engaged in the ILO and by those other international organizations. Yet there remains a continuing debate about the changing role of the ILO amongst informed commentators.

The ILO's work program around the crisis echoed the conclusions to Chapter 6, which identified the importance for the "new" ILO of working with other international organizations. The "new" ILO, and its principles and strategies, remain the focus of intense debate, to which we now turn.

8 Concluding thoughts
Whither the ILO?

In 2009, the ILO celebrated its 90th year. Outliving the League of Nations and the re-creation of international institutions after the Second World War, the ILO is a remarkable survivor. We have argued that this success is due to a number of factors. Effective leadership, the ability to adapt to changing circumstances, and relevance in an area of international importance have been particularly important. Globalization, and the emergence of global regulation as a consequence, provides a contemporary context offering the ILO many opportunities to maintain its role and status, Yet, at the same time, that context is not easy for the ILO. As global regulation emerges, other international institutions have taken up the issue of labor standards, potentially threatening the unique role of the ILO. Moreover, the corporate world has done the same as it seeks, on the one hand, to defend its market position against accusation of labor market exploitation and, on the other, builds labor (and other) standards into its brands. The ILO now faces competition on its traditional turf.

The ILO also comes under assault from other directions. Commentaries challenge its relevance, organizational structure, priorities, representativity and many other aspects of its existence. Some of those criticisms have emerged from within the organization, perhaps lending weight to their charges. We offer here our assessment of the ILO and its critics.

Trying to order the various criticisms of the ILO is not easy, as they often overlap and repeat each other. Thus, for example, at the most trite level, there is constant reference to the inability of the ILO to enforce its conventions and recommendations. Moral suasion, linked on relatively rare occasions with "naming and shaming," is for some easily dismissed as a sign of the ILO's essential weakness. The response from the ILO might be threefold, First, ratifications increase in number as countries, at least formally, adopt ILO standards. Second, an ILO version of gunboat diplomacy would not establish better labor conditions in any case. Countries, and the social partners within countries, must understand the benefits of, and want to see set in place, good labor standards. In any jurisdiction, it is always preferable to have standards observed as a matter of course, rather than as an effect of a policing regime. In an ideal world, enforcement is required in exceptional cases. Third, as an international institution, based on the decisions of the social partners, the ILO is properly tied to the outcomes of the social partners' deliberations. Even the strong epistemic community within the ILO is limited in the extent that it can push the envelope created by those deliberations.

There are, however, positions critical of the ILO, which merit careful consideration. In somewhat arbitrary fashion, noting the point about overlapping perspectives made above, we suggest that there are four bodies of thought of note. They are:

- The Social Movement Internationalism school (for example, the criticism of the ILO offered by Peter Waterman);[1]
- The Strategic Misdirection school (for example, Standing, Alston, Alston and Heenan);[2]
- The Organizational Challenges school (for example, Hagen, Vosko, Prugl, Cooney);[3] and
- The ILO school (for example, Langille and Maupain[4] as well as the speeches and statements by Somavia).

The Social Movement Internationalism school

This school of thought is defined by its powerful criticism of contemporary capitalist accumulation. It promotes, in response, social movement unionism, which rejects traditional modes of trade union organization and looks to unions to move into political alliance with broader social movements in society. The goal is transformation of the capitalist system, based on a global political reach grounded in myriad local social movement activities and agencies. Trade unions must be emancipated if they are to play a progressive role in that transformation. Institutions such as the International Trade Union Confederation (ITUC) and the ILO are construed as being committed neither to that transformation, nor to the required emancipation of the trade unions.

In this view, the ILO, by focusing on development issues and, more recently, by accepting the existence of globalization (an acceptance explicit in Hansenne's commentaries, for example), has contributed to the "disarming" of working people as they face the effects of contemporary, dynamic and aggressive capitalism. The ILO faces a "crisis of identity." Because it has never been able to enforce its conventions, it has relied on rhetoric, and, as capitalism has become more aggressive as it globalizes, that level of rhetoric has simply increased in response to the ILO's impotence. The upshot is that the ILO needs to reinvent itself if it is to be of any relevance to working people internationally.

This is a serious criticism of the ILO, about which we will say a little, as it has not featured hitherto in our discussion. It has been a criticism of the ILO since its inception. The ILO has never been an agency for the transformation of capitalism. As we noted earlier, it was created of the capitalist system and operates within it. Its "political" rationale was initially to respond to the threat of radical worker mobilization, and it became, over time, a pluralist institution in which the tripartite partners, in unique fashion, meet and deliberate. The social movement internationalism perspective is, equally, a criticism of the international trade union movement, for the latter has been enmeshed in the tripartite structures of the ILO since 1919. Yet this reflects, first, the reality that trade unions are themselves the product of capitalism; second, if some trade unions perceive themselves as agents of capitalism's overthrow, most do not; third, trade unions choose to engage in the ILO process. Indeed, in many countries with multiple trade union centers, there is competition to be the worker representative in the ILO.

For the social movement internationalist tradition, the key to a transformed ILO (or its complete marginalization) lies in the union movement's capacity to reorientate the international union movement to social movement politics. It is unlikely that the social partners engaged with the ILO will be influenced greatly by the social movement tradition, except insofar as engagement with NGOs on a more structured basis is likely. In turn, the social movement tradition expects to see declining global trade union densities and, perhaps, suggest that the emperor's clothes are increasingly threadbare.

The Strategic Misdirection school

We have discussed this tradition at some length in Chapter 4 and made other references to it. Standing, and Alston (and Heenan) are not arguing precisely aligned cases. Standing's argument shares some of the concerns about the ILO found in the social movement internationalist tradition. In particular, Standing's view, and the manner of its statement, that misdirection occurred long before 1994, and that the ILO post-1994, and particularly post-1999, has adopted positions which "(correspond) with a neo liberal economic view of protective regulations" could find a home in Waterman's commentary. However, in broad terms, this tradition agrees that the post-1994 refocusing of the ILO has been sorely misdirected, to the detriment of the ILO and the role that it should play. But what is to be done about this misdirection? Standing concludes his frank dissection of the contemporary ILO with a weary belief that it will survive, not because of its good works, but because "[t]he Global Transformation yearns for a body establishing and inducing implementation of rules, 'codes of conduct' and Conventions promoting equitable practices." Meanwhile, he argues, the technical strengths of the ILO will wither. Finally, he suggests "[t]he organization is a testament to the past century of labors trying to protect employees in the standard employment relationship. Like it or not, in the early twenty-first century, labor *is* a commodity. And the ILO cannot do much about it." This must be, for Standing, a deeply depressing conclusion, as he spent, until 2006, more than 30 years working as a highly respected and senior staff member of the ILO and was a member of Somavia's transitional team. Standing seems to hold out little hope for the reassertion of a strong and effective ILO able to defend labor's interests.

Alston and Heenan echo much of Standing's concern about the post-1994 ILO model when they write:

> In essence, our thesis is that the concept and practice of international labour standards, implemented within a framework established in the 1920s and subsequently developed and overseen by the ILO, has, in the space of only ten years, been systematically superceded by a nebulous, open-ended, and essentially self-defined and self-evaluated system of so-called core labor standards.[5]

Their answer is a stronger, flexible ILO, still rooted in labor rights. As they put it:

> A truly international system, built around a strong and flexible ILO, is the one that is best capable of delivering a package of labour rights which can truly be said to satisfy the requirements of international human rights standards. This includes a clear and uniform catalogue of rights, entitlement to which does not depend on geographical position or industry (especially freedom of association), an independent assessment of what matters should be regulated, an independent review of disputes, a broader conception of labour regulation in order to distinguish the employment contract from other commercial contracts, and the opportunity to raise labour standards in line with development and wealth.[6]

Alston and Heenan recognize well where the criticism of their view will come from. In particular, they recognize that global circumstances required the ILO to change. The problem for them was that the change was in the wrong direction. One response to their argument is, of course, wait and see. The post-1994 shifts in the ILO are in place and are unlikely to be unraveled. Nobody expects, or wants, a return to the ILO of the 1960s. Consensus amongst the social partners surrounds the post-1994 model, so it is also, warts and all, legitimate.

There is another dimension of this criticism that should be considered. As we have noted, Standing was a long-time and respected staff member of the ILO. His criticism owes something to existing and past ILO staffers. Standing may well speak, deliberately or not, for elements within the factionalized micro-politics of the ILO, disaffected with the post-1994 change process. Organizational change is always fraught, and adverse commentaries consequent on organizational change may reflect many different currents and perspectives. This is also true for Alston, and Alston and Heenan, who speak from the labor rights perspective. As is to be expected, the analytical discussion in and around the ILO is itself fragmented, with technical and specialist labor lawyers enjoying a status commensurate with the traditional status of labor law in the ILO. The post-1994 changes in the ILO downplay the labor rights perspective as a broader social justice approach is extended across the ILO work plan. The Strategic Misdirection school may reflect the intellectual and organizational tensions that follow from that refocusing.

The Organizational Challenges school

Cooney and Hagen represent an almost secular criticism of the ILO as an organization, for they are driven particularly by neither deep disquiet about the post-1994 change process, nor concern about any long-term commitment to capitalist accumulation. They are, however, seized of some organizational and structural issues, which dog the ILO and may grow in significance. Cooney argues that the ILO suffers from three key flaws. The first is distorted representation. Neither employer nor trade union representation reflects the true global make-up of their respective constituencies. Trade union representation reflects a declining percentage of global labor, whilst employers simply fail to capture the needs of key groups, such as the self-employed and home workers. In sum, representation in the ILO has not kept up with the changing profiles of employers and employees in the global economy. Second, overtaxing procedures imposed by the ILO across increasing numbers of reporting requirements has resulted in member states being unable, or unwilling, to report properly on ILO-related matters. Third, evaluation and monitoring have been poorly developed in the ILO such that the social consequences of ILO activities are difficult to measure and understand. The post-1994 reforms in the ILO have, Cooney argues, done little about the three flaws. It should be noted that he was writing in 1999, so was not able to comment on the managerial and strategic reforms introduced by Somavia, which were designed to meet some of the problems identified in Cooney's second and third flaws.

Cooney proposed a range of remedies to deal with these flaws. They included better evaluation and monitoring, improved prioritization of activities, greater inclusivity in ILO activities (for example, increased involvement of NGOs), reformed representation, improved incentives for states considering the implementation of ILO-derived measures, and more analytical work to define the ILO's approach to global labor problems.

Hagen, like Standing, a one-time senior staff member in the ILO, identified three problems facing the ILO. The first was a crisis of identity, similar to the argument made about distorted representation by Cooney. Hagen identified the need on the part of the ILO to respond to civil society (NGOs particularly). She too highlighted the limited representativity of employer and trade union organizations in the ILO and argued that incumbents will act in a self-interested way. The second crisis was one of effectiveness. This addresses the issues of enforcement and cumbersome procedures, and is again at one with Cooney's analysis. However, as Hagen was writing in 2003, she was able to factor into her account the changes introduced by Somavia and by the follow-up procedures associated with the 1998 declaration. Third was the crisis of relevance. The ILO is no longer the only agency looking at standards. Moreover, in some cases (minimum wages, occupational health and safety, for example) the attempt to improve relevance by defining core labor standards has in fact marginalized very important standards, which occur as high priorities in other orderings of core standards. On the other hand, in the case of some core standards defined after 1994, the question must be asked whether they are entirely achievable. In asking these questions, Hagen was casting a critical spotlight over the post-1994 definition of core standards, whilst in general seeing the post-1994 refocusing in a positive light.

The Organizational Challenge school is important, for much of its commentary is as important after the 1994 reforms as before, and it is designed, on the whole, to be constructive criticism. They are not fundamentally questioning the ILO's existence. Indeed, they generally support its activities and much of what they write could be seen as supportive of Somavia's own agenda for change in the ILO. Broad representation, relevance, efficient process, effective evaluation and monitoring, and careful assessment of what is "core" and what is not are examples of issues any director-general would take seriously.

The ILO school

We do not propose to repeat the discussion of Maupain and Langille provided in Chapter 4. Nor will we review again the rationale for either Hansenne's or Somavia's refocusing of the ILO. It is, however, important to set against the previous schools the existence of a school of thought in and around the ILO sympathetic to the post-1994 refocusing. The gist of its thinking is that the ILO faced dramatically changed circumstances, to which it had failed to react. In this view, the ILO must change or become irrelevant. The ILO responded by refocusing its efforts in ways which draw substantially on previous intellectual and organizational strengths, but also repositioning the ILO as the "global social pillar." Labor rights continued to be central to the ILO mission, but in ways which tied them much more effectively to a broader social justice agenda. The extraordinary technical abilities of the ILO remained central to the ILO's success. Co-operation with other international agencies was promoted as a vital way to achieve successful outcomes, as was the political support needed to promote Somavia's call for greater policy coherence. The ILO was organizationally better equipped in terms of positioning and performance management to push forward its strategic agenda. The traditional ILO approach on promotion and encouragement remains in place and stands as a fundamental pillar of its institutional activities. For the ILO school, post-1994 was not only necessary and a success but also the contemporary manifestation of an organization whose history demonstrates an ability to adapt to the needs of the time and reflect growing concerns with the social costs of globalization.

A fifth option: the ILO and the International Labor Standards Regime

There is a fifth analysis of the ILO, which places the ILO in the emerging framework of global governance.[7] Developing an analysis of the ILO derived initially from the international relations and international political economy literatures on regimes and global governance, this approach suggests that the ILO is the center of a global regime of labor standards (the International Labor Standards Regime), in which the ILO constitutes simultaneously the institutional presence of the regime, and also the process in which the norms, values and decision-making procedures associated with the International Labor Standards Regime are observed.

This approach has something in common with the Social Movement Internationalism school, in that it is predicated on a view that global economic integration inevitably requires global political governance, in which the balance of power between contending social, political and economic constituencies will be hard-fought. In this view, global governance will include a platform of labor standards and, also, a social protection dimension. The precise configuration of both is still indeterminate, as global governance is a changing feast, very much still in formation. However, in this analysis, the ILO, since its creation, has been developing its global role in order to become a key player, if not the key player, in the definition of, first, those standards and, second, the social protection framework of the global order.

The import of this analysis has much in common with the analyses of globalization offered by Hansenne and Somavia. The post-1994 repositioning of the ILO has taken as a central theme the need for the ILO to position itself in an emerging global order. Repositioning has required institutional change in the ILO to meet new circumstances, a greater recognition of the interactions, needed and inevitable, between international agencies, and the development of new interventions and agendas to respond to changing circumstances. However, that repositioning is based on the long years of experience and presence, which have established the ILO as a major international agency.

That repositioning encompasses many of the key features of the post-1994 model. Here are three examples, illustrative but not comprehensive. First, labor standards will not remain solely in the charge of the ILO. The extension of labor standards at global level will mean other agencies, including private sector bodies, will adopt them (as in, for example, CSR initiatives). The ILO might well see this as a success, rather than as a threat. The priority attached to the ILO's knowledge base in labor standards, and its primacy as the defender of labor standards, is not substantially threatened by that extension. Rather, the ILO is in a position to influence far wider debates about the form and intent of labor standards.

Second, the ILO's role in the broader social protection debate is likely to grow, and it may seem that, as a consequence, the labor standards dimension of ILO activities is in relative decline. This may be an opportunity, rather than a threat. Since the Declaration of Philadelphia in particular, the ILO has claimed an international role beyond labor standards setting. In practice, the ILO's emerging role in global governance is likely to provide opportunity for the ILO to build its role in both standard-setting and broader social protection policy development.

Third, traditional ILO tripartism offers a useful mechanism for global engagement of many voices in global governance. As global governance becomes a reality, the question of representation in its institutions and decision-making will become a significant political issue, and whilst it may not be the only representative mechanism adopted, it is likely to play an important role not only in the International Labor Standards Regime, but also in other locations of global decision-making.

Conclusion

The ILO has survived, perhaps against the odds, despite the fact that there have been many times in its 90 years when its future has looked uncertain, or international or social partner support has waned, or when financial vicissitude has made program delivery difficult. Despite its rocky start in the doomed League of Nations and other challenges, it is now, arguably, as strong an organization as it has ever been. Its survival has rested on strong, strategic leadership, an ability to reposition itself strategically, and a cadre of very competent technical staff providing relevant, high-quality advice. Above all, however, labor standards and social protection matter in an increasingly integrated global economy. The ILO's unswerving commitment to both is a major factor in its survival and its current high profile. It will be a role that is likely to grow in the future.

Select bibliography

Antony Alcock, *The History of the International Labour Organisation* (London: Octagon Press, 1971) remains an important account of the origins and development of the ILO until the 1960s.

Anthony Endres and Grant Fleming, *International Organizations and the Analysis of Economic Policy* (Cambridge: Cambridge University Press, 2002) offers the most detailed examination of the contribution by ILO staff to economic thought and policy in the inter-war period.

Gary Fields, *Trade and Labour Standards: A Review of the Issues* (Paris: OECD, 1995) provides an economist's take on the Social Clause debate.

Nigel Haworth and Steve Hughes, "From Marrakesh to Doha and beyond: The Tortuous Progress of the Contemporary Trade and Labour Standards Debate," in *The Politics of International Trade*, ed. Dominic Kelly and Wyn Grant (London: Palgrave, 2004) traces the progress of the Social Clause from the end of the Uruguay Round of the GATT.

Nigel Haworth, Steve Hughes, and Rorden Wilkinson, "The International Labour Standards Regime: A Case Study in Global Regulation," *Environment and Planning A* 37, no. 11 (2005): 1939–53 is an analytical account of the ILO in the context of global governance.

B. Hepple, "Rights at Work," in *Decent Work: Objectives and Strategies*, ed. Dharam Ghai (Geneva: IILS-ILO, 2006), 33–76 is a helpful commentary in what is a complex and often difficult discussion on the contemporary debates around the definition of core labor standards and their incorporation into the Declaration on Fundamental Principles and Rights at Work.

International Labour Organization, the Director-General's reports to the International Labour Conference and to the Governing Body of the ILO are a good source on the Somavia period. They can be found on the ILO's webpage at: www.ilo.org/global/lang-en/index.htm

The International Labour Review is the ILO's flagship journal, established in 1921, and recently re-vamped and re-launched with a new editor and editorial board. It is printed in English, French and Spanish, and provides general material on the ILO and its activities and thinking.

Carol Riegelman Lubin and Ann Winslow, *Social Justice for Women. The International Labour Organisation* (Durham, N.C.: Duke University Press,

1990) provides a detailed and readable analysis of the important role women played in the establishment of the ILO and its subsequent attempts in promoting justice for women.

David A. Morse, *The Origin and Evolution of the ILO and Its Role in the World Community* (Ithaca, N.Y.: Cornell University Press, 1969) written by a previous director-general, this is an interesting account of the ILO from a participant's perspective.

G. Rodgers, E. Lee, L. Swepston and J. van Daele, *The ILO and the Quest for Social Justice 1919–2009* (Geneva: International Labour Office, 2009) is one of two important recent volumes on the ILO. It was written as part of the ILO "Century Project," which aims to document and analyze the 100 years of ILO activity in the run up to its centenary in 2019. The authors offer a comprehensive commentary on the history of the ILO and also provide a bibliography of contributions to the "Century Project."

M. Rodriguez, J. van Daele, M. van der Linden, and G. van Goethem, eds., *The International Labour Organization: Historical Explorations* (Bern: Peter Lang, 2010) is the other recent important volume, offering contributions from around the world examining the global reach of the ILO in its pursuit of social justice.

W. Sengenberger, *The Role and Impact of International Labour Standards; A Report Prepared for the Friedrich-Ebert-Stiftung* (Bonn: Friedrich-Ebert-Stiftung, Global Trade Union Programme, 2005) presents a sympathetic view of the impact of labor standards in relation to the Social Clause debate.

World Commission on the Social Dimension of Globalization, "A Fair Globalisation: Creating Opportunities for All" (Geneva: International Labour Office, 2004) is a report providing background against which to situate the post-1994 refocusing of the ILO, and, in particular, the focus provided by Juan Somavia.

Notes

Foreword

1 See Rorden Wilkinson, "Peripheralising Labour: The ILO, WTO and the Completion of the Bretton Woods Project," in Jeffery Harrod and Robert O'Brien, eds., *Globalized Unions? Theory and Strategies of Organized Labour in the Global Political Economy* (London: Routledge, 2002), 204–20; and "Labour and Trade-Related Regulation: Beyond the Trade-Labour Standards Debate?" *British Journal of Politics and International Relations* 1, no. 2 (June 1999): 165–91.
2 Nigel Haworth and Stephen Hughes, "Trade and International Labour Standards: issues and debates over a social clause," *Journal of Industrial Relations* 39, no. 2 (1997): 179–95.
3 For a summary of works on the ILO see Jasmien van Daele, "The International Labour Organization (ILO) in Past and Present Research," *International Review of Social History* 53, no. 3 (2008): 485–511.
4 The two most significant full length works on the ILO are: John W. Follows, *Antecedents of the International Labour Organization* (Oxford: Clarendon Press, 1951); and Anthony Alcock, *History of the International Labor Organization* (New York: Octagon Books, 1971).
5 Robert Cox is the most notable exception. See Robert W. Cox, "The Idea of International Labour Regulation," *International Labour Review* 68, no. 2 (1953): 191–96; and "Labor and Hegemony," *International Organization* 31, no. 3 (1977): 385–424.
6 For instance, the Security Council is routinely subjected to the use of analytical fine-tooth combs. For an encyclopedic treatment since 1945 see Vaughan Lowe, Adam Roberts, Jennifer Welsh and Dominik Zaum, eds., *The United Nations Security Council and War: The Evolution of Thought and Practice since 1945* (Oxford: Oxford University Press, 2008). See the analysis of one decision by Michael N. Barnett, "The UN Security Council, Indifference, and Genocide in Rwanda," *Cultural Anthropology* 12, no. 4 (1997): 511–78; as well as his longer *Eyewitness to a Genocide: The United Nations and Rwanda* (Ithaca, N.Y.: Cornell University Press, 2002). For a brief history of the institution, see Edward C. Luck's contribution to this series, *The UN Security Council*, 2nd ed. (London: Routledge, 2010).

Introduction

1 See ILO, "IMF Managing-Director Calls for Greater Co-operation with the ILO," 23 March 2009 (available at: www.ilo.org/global/About_the_ILO/ Media_and_public_information).

1 A brief history of the ILO

1 Edward Phelan, *Yes and Albert Thomas* (London: Cresset Press, 1936), 13–17. See also Antony Alcock, *History of the International Labour Organization* (London: Macmillan, 1971).
2 Alcock, *History of the International Labour Organization*, 41–42.
3 Wilfred Jenks, "Introduction to the personal memoirs of Edward Phelan," in *Edward Phelan and the ILO: Life and Views of an International Social Actor* (Geneva: International Labour Office, 2009).
4 Victor-Yves Ghebali, *The International Labor Organization: A Case Study on the Evolution of U.N. Specialized Agencies* (London: Martinus Nijhoff Publishers, 1989), 16.
5 See, Gary Ostrower, "The American Decision to Join the International Labour Organization," *Labor History* 16, no. 4 (1975): 495–504. Also, Alcock, *History of the International Labour Organization*, 119.
6 J. K. Galbraith, *The Great Crash 1929* (Harmondsworth: Penguin, 1975), 30.
7 As the United States was still not a member of the ILO the delegation was given observer status. Nonetheless despite the absence of an employer representative it was an important precedent for both the United States and the ILO.
8 As secretary of labor and a close friend of Roosevelt, Perkins was the most influential advocate of ILO membership in the Roosevelt administration.
9 Ostrower, "The American Decision to Join the International Labour Organization," 499.
10 Alcock, *History of the International Labour Organization*, 99.
11 Edward Phelan, "Some Reminiscences of the International Labour Organization," *Studies, An Irish Critical Quarterly* 14 (1954): 243.
12 Phelan, "Some Reminiscences of the International Labour Organization," 249.
13 Harold Butler, *The Lost Peace* (London: Faber and Faber, 1941), 52.
14 Butler, *The Lost Peace*, 54.
15 R. F. Holland, *European Decolonisation 1918–1981: An Introductory Survey* (Basingstoke: Macmillan, 1985), 134.
16 Eric Hobsbawm, *Age of Extremes: The Short Twentieth Century 1914–1991* (London: Abacus, 1995), 108.
17 Ernst Hass, *Beyond the Nation State: Functionalism and International Organization* (Stanford, Calif.: Stanford University Press, 1964).
18 Robert Cox, "Labor and Hegemony," *International Organization* 31 (Summer 1977): 402.
19 The United States stopped paying its contributions in 1970, causing significant financial difficulty for the ILO. Subsequently, in 1975, the United States gave two years' notice of the intention to leave the ILO, which occurred in 1977. The United States rejoined the ILO in 1980.
20 Standing offers an analysis of the period around the formation of the Washington Consensus and what he sees as the lost opportunities for the ILO in that period and subsequently. See Guy Standing, "The ILO: An Agency for Globalisation?" *Development and Change* 39, no 3 (2008): 355–84.

21 See *Proposed ILO Declaration on Social Justice for a Fair Globalisation*, International Labour Conference, 97th session, Geneva 2008.

2 Structure and organization of the ILO

1 The ILO webpage at www.ilo.org/global/lang-en/index.htm contains a wealth of material about the structure and procedures of the ILO.
2 See United States Department of Labor at www.dol.gov/ilab/programs/oir/ILO.htm
3 Multilateral Organisation Performance Assessment Network, *Donor Perceptions of Multilateral Partnerships at Country Level Annual Survey* (MOPAN, 2006), 20–29. www.mopanonline.org

3 The ILO and globalization

1 We have accepted, for the purposes of this text, the generic notion of globalization, whilst recognizing the force of the critique offered against the concept.
2 The Washington Consensus is used by some commentators as a synonym for "market fundamentalism." Thus, it has a narrow meaning, that is, the specific policy recommendations that the international financial institutions, inter alia, adopted (for example, fiscal restraint, reduced public expenditure, privatization, trade liberalization and so on), and a broader meaning, that is, the generic market fundamentalist approach.
3 We use the notion of "modern" social democracy as a short-hand term to denote social democratic governments, which have come to power since the widespread adoption of neo-liberal approaches to economic governance, that is, since the early 1970s, and which seek to respond at national level to both the impact of globalization and the global reach of neo-liberal economic policies.
4 Guy Standing, "The ILO: An Agency for Globalization?" *Development and Change* 39, no. 3 (2008): 355–84.
5 The United States rejoined the ILO in 1980.
6 ILO, *Defending Values, Promoting Change: Social Justice in a Global Economy: An ILO Agenda*, Report of the director-general to the International Labour Conference, 81st session, Geneva 1994.
7 For controversy, see Standing, "The ILO: An Agency for Globalization?" 378.
8 ILO, *A Fair Globalisation: Creating Opportunities for All* (Geneva: ILO, 2004).
9 ILO, *A Fair Globalisation: The Role of the ILO, Report of the Director-General on the World Commission on the Social Dimension of Globalisation*, Report of the director-general to the International Labour Conference, 92nd Session, Geneva 2004.
10 Decent Work is discussed in detail in Chapter 6.

4 The Declaration on Fundamental Principles and Rights at Work: a new approach to labor standards?

1 ILO, *The ILO, Standard Setting and Globalization*, Report of the director-general to the International Labour Conference, 85th Session, Geneva 1997.

2 Katherine Hagen, *The International Labor Organization: Can It Deliver the Social Dimension of Globalization?* (Geneva: Friedrich-Ebert-Stiftung, Occasional Papers, 11, 2003).
3 ILO, *The ILO, Standard Setting and Globalization*.
4 See also, for example, ILO, *Follow-up on the Discussion of the Report of the Director-General to the 85th Session (1997) of the International Labour Conference*, Governing Body 1997 (GB 270/3/1, GB 270/3/2); ILO, *Draft of a Possible Declaration of Principles Concerning Fundamental Rights and Its Appropriate Follow-up for Consideration at the 86th Session (1998) of the International Labour Conference*, Governing Body 1998 (GB 271/3/1).
5 ILO, *ILO Declaration on Fundamental Principles and Rights at Work*, International Labour Conference, 86th Session, Geneva 1998.
6 ILO, *ILO Programme Implementation 2006–07*, Report of the director-general to the International Labour Conference, 97th Session, Geneva 2008.
7 Hagen, *The International Labor Organization: Can It Deliver the Social Dimension of Globalization*, 12.
8 Guy Standing, "The ILO: An Agency for Globalization?," *Development and Change* 39, no. 3 (2008): 355–84. F. Maupain, "Revitalization Not Retreat: The Real Potential of the 1998 ILO Declaration for the Universal Protection of Workers' Rights," *European Journal of International Law* 16, no. 3 (2005): 439–65. The key elements of the Alston, Heenan and Langille debate take the following sequence: P. Alston and J. Heenan, "Shrinking the International Labor Code: An Unintended Consequence of the 1998 ILO Declaration on Fundamental Principles and Rights at Work?" *New York University Journal of International Law and Politics* 36 (2004): 221–64; "Core Labor Standards and the Transformation of the International Labor Rights Regime," *European Journal of International Law* 15, no. 3 (2004): 457–521; Brian Langille, "Core Labor Rights: The True Story (Reply to Alston)," *European Journal of International Law* 16, no. 3 (2005): 409–37; and P. Alston, "Facing Up to the Complexities of the ILO's Core Labor Standards Agenda," *European Journal of International Law* 16, no. 3 (2005): 467–80.
9 For a broadly sympathetic understanding of rights at work under the post-1998 model see B.Hepple, "Rights at Work," in Darim Ghai, ed., *Decent Work: Objectives and Strategies* (Geneva: IILS-ILO, 2006), 33–76.
10 Maupain, "Revitalization Not Retreat: The Real Potential of the 1998 ILO Declaration for the Universal Protection of Workers' Rights." At the time of writing, Maupain and Langille are the obvious counterpoint to Standing and Alston and Alston and Heenan. The stronger tone of the critique offered by Standing, in his article and also in published interviews, will inevitably produce a response from the ILO. Note also Alston's reply to Langille, which does little to temper the tone of the debate.
11 See Langille, "Core Labor Rights: The True Story (Reply to Alston)."

5 The ILO and the WTO: the tortuous case of the Social Clause

1 Freedom of association and collective bargaining (Conventions 87 and 98); Abolition of forced labor (Conventions 29 and 105); Prevention of discrimination in employment and equal pay for work of equal value (Conventions

111 and 100); Minimum age for the employment of children (Convention 138); and Against the most extreme form of child labor (Convention 182). Note that four other conventions have been denoted as "priority" conventions by the ILO's Governing Body. They are: Labor Inspection Convention, 1947 (no. 81); Labor Inspection (Agriculture) Convention, 1969 (no. 129); Tripartite Consultation (International Labor Standards) Convention, 1976 (no. 144); and Employment Policy Convention, 1964 (no. 122).

2 Gary Fields, *Trade and Labor Standards: A Review of the Issues* (Paris: OECD, 1995); US Department of Labor, Bureau of International Labor Affairs, *International Labor Standards and Global Economic Integration: Proceedings of a Symposium* (Washington, DC: US Department of Labor, 1994); Dani Rodrik, "Labor Standards in International Trade: Do They Matter and What Do We Do About Them?," in *Emerging Agenda for Global Trade: High Stakes for Developing Countries*, eds. Robert Lawrence, Dani Rodrik, and John Whalley (Washington, DC: Overseas Development Council, 1996); Andre Sapir, "The Interaction Between Labor Standards and International Trade Policy," *The World Economy* 18 (1995): 791–803; T. N. Srinivasan, "International Trade and Labor Standards," in *Challenges to the New World Trade Organization*, eds. Pitou van Dijck and Gerrit Faber (Amsterdam: Martinus Nijhoff/Kluwer, 1995); W. Sengenberger and D. Campbell, eds., *International Labour Standards and Economic Interdependence* (Geneva: International Labour Organization, 1994); and W. Sengenberger, *The Role and Impact of International Labor Standards: A Report Prepared for the Friedrich-Ebert-Stiftung* (Bonn: Friedrich-Ebert Stiftung, Global Trade Union Programme, 2005).

3 ILO, *ILO Declaration on Fundamental Principles and Rights at Work*, International Labour Conference, 86th Session, Geneva 1998.

4 ILO, *Continuation of Discussions Concerning the Programme of Work and Mandate of the Working Party*, Working Party on the Social Dimensions of the Liberalization of International Trade, Governing Body 1997 (GB.268/WP/SDL/1/3).

5 World Trade Organization, *Singapore Ministerial Declaration*, 1996, (WT/MIN(96)/DEC/W. 13 December), para. 4.

6 N. Jansen and E. Lee, *Trade and Employment: Challenges for Policy Research* (Geneva: WTO and ILO, 2007).

7 ILO, *Trade and Employment: Follow-up to the Joint ILO/WTO Secretariat Study*, Working Party on the Social Dimensions of the Liberalization of International Trade, Governing Body 2007 (GB.300/WP/SDG/2).

8 ILO, *Director-General's Report to Governing Body*, Governing Body 1994, (GB.261/WP/SDL/1).

9 ILO, *The ILO, Standard Setting and Globalization*, Report of the director-general to the International Labour Conference, 85th Session, Geneva 1997.

10 ILO, *The ILO, Standard Setting and Globalization*, 10.

11 Fieldwork carried out by the authors in the ILO in the 1990s confirmed this view. Senior ILO staff made it clear that they feared any success that the Social Clause might have in the WTO system. Those fears were expressed in terms of a possible threat to the status of the ILO, and to specialist knowledge and functions embodied in the ILO staff.

12 A helpful and brief commentary on enforcement, if now a little dated, is that offered by K. Elliott, *The ILO and the Enforcement of Core Labor*

Notes 111

    Standards, International Economics Policy Brief no. 00–06, Institute for International Economics, Washington, DC, 2000.
13 The relevant committee is the Committee of Experts on the Application of Conventions and Recommendations.
14 The Conference Committee on the Application of Conventions and Recommendations.
15 In this Hansenne is quite correct. The founding principles of the ILO in 1919 sought to avoid imposition of outcomes and there were relatively few complaints taken up by the ILO in its first years. In fact, there have been relatively few complaints lodged over the life of the ILO.
16 Nigel Haworth and Steve Hughes, "Under Scrutiny, the ECA, the ILO and the NZCTU complaint. 1993–95," *New Zealand Journal of Industrial Relations* 20, no. 2 (August 1995): 143–61. Also, when Somavia named countries adversely as a result of the follow-up to the declaration, he attracted considerable criticism from not only the named countries but also others fearing that one day they might be named.
17 Nigel Haworth and Steve Hughes, *Death of a Social Clause*, Manchester Papers in Politics, 3/00, Department of Government, Manchester University, 2000. See also Nigel Haworth and Steve Hughes, "From Marrakech to Doha and Beyond: The Tortuous Progress of the Contemporary Trade and Labour Standards Debate," in *The Politics of International Trade in the Twenty First Century*, eds. D. Kelly and W. Grant (Basingstoke: Palgrave, 2005); and Nigel Haworth and Steve Hughes, "Trade Liberalisation and the ILO: Whither the Social Clause?" in *Current Research in Industrial Relations in Australia and New Zealand*, eds. R. Fells and T. Todd (Perth, WA: AIRRANZ, 1996).

6 Decent Work, Fair Globalisation, and strategic planning: Somavia's ILO

1 United Nations, *Final Report of the World Summit for Social Development* (Copenhagen: United Nations, 1995).
2 ILO, *A Fair Globalisation: Creating Opportunities for All* (Geneva: ILO, 2004).
3 ILO, *Decent Work*, Report of the director-general, International Labour Conference, 87th Session, Geneva 1999.
4 For an overview of the ILO discussion, see Darim Ghai, *Decent Work: Objectives and Strategies* (Geneva: IILS-ILO, 2006). For a developed statement by Somavia of the potential in Decent Work, see ILO, *Reducing the Decent Work Deficit*, Report of the director-general, International Labour Conference, 89th Session, Geneva 2001.
5 ILO, *Reducing the Decent Work Deficit*, Report of the director-general, 13.
6 ILO, *Reducing the Decent Work Deficit*, Report of the director-general, 4.
7 The eight countries were Bahrain, Bangladesh, Denmark, Ghana, Kazakhstan, Morocco, Panama, and the Philippines. See Azita Awad, "Decent Work as a National Goal: The Experience of the Decent Work Pilot Programme (DWPP) and Other Related Initiatives," 2nd South-East Asia and the Pacific Subregional Tripartite Forum on Decent Work, Melbourne, Australia, April 2005. See also the ILO's DWPP at www.ilo.org/public/english/bureau/dwpp.
8 In Ethiopia, Ghana, Honduras, Mali, Sudan, Tanzania; Cambodia, Indonesia, Nepal, Pakistan, Viet Nam; Kyrgyzstan; Bolivia, Ecuador, Peru and Yemen.

112 Notes

9 Awad, "Decent Work as a National Goal."
10 Graeme Buckley, *Decent Work in a Least Developed Economy: A Critical Assessment of the Ethiopia PRSP*, Geneva: Working Paper no. 42, Policy Integration Department, National Policy Group, International Labour Office, July 2004.
11 ILO, *ILO Decent Work Country Programmes: A Guidebook* (Geneva: ILO, 2005).
12 ILO, *ILO Programme Implementation*, Report of the director-general, International Labour Conference, 97th Session, Geneva 2008.
13 The designation "declaration 2008" will refer to the Declaration on Social Justice for a Fair Globalization in order to distinguish it from the Declaration on Fundamental Principles and Rights at Work, referred to simply as "the declaration."
14 Originally the Working Party on the Social Dimensions of the Liberalization of International Trade, established in 1994. Discussions in 1999 and 2000 led to its renaming as the Working Party on the Social Dimensions of Globalization in 2000. The rationale was to link the ILO's work on the social dimensions of globalization with that of other international agencies on a basis that extended beyond trade-related issues. See ILO, *Future Activities of the Working Party*, Governing Body 2000 (GB.277/WP/SDL/1).
15 ILO, *A Fair Globalisation: the Role of the ILO: Report of the Director-General on the World Commission on the Social Dimension of Globalisation*, Report of the director-general to the International Labour Conference, 92nd Session, Geneva 2004.
16 ILO, *Programme and Budget proposals for 2000–01: Approval of the Detailed Budget and Further Development of Strategic Budgeting*, Governing Body 1999 (GB.276/PFA/9); and ILO, *Strategic Policy Framework, 2002–05, and Preview of the Programme and Budget Proposals for 2002–03*, Governing Body 2000 (GB.279/PFA/6).
17 ILO, *Strategic Policy Framework 2010–2015 and Preview of the Programme and Budget Proposals 2010–2011*, Governing Body 2008 (GB.303/PFA/2). The PSF was originally introduced in 2000. See also ILO, *Strategic Policy Framework, 2002–05*.
18 Guy Standing, "The ILO: An Agency for Globalisation?" *Development and Change* 39, no. 3 (2008): 355–84.
19 Author interview.
20 Brian Langille, "Core Labor Rights, The True Story (Reply to Alston)," *European Journal of International Law* 16, no. 3 (2005): 409–37.
21 Author interviews.

7 The ILO at work in the 2007 global economic crisis

1 A. Blundell-Wignall, P. Atkinson, and S. Lee, *The Current Financial Crisis: Causes and Policy Issues* (Paris: OECD, Financial Market Trends, 2008).
2 World Bank, *Global Financial Crisis and Impact on Developing Countries* (Washington, DC: World Bank Global Monitoring Report, 2009).
3 ILO, *"Protecting People, Promoting Jobs": A Survey of Country Employment and Social Protection Policy Responses to the Global Economic Crisis; An ILO Report to the G20 Leaders' Summit*, G20 leaders' meeting, Pittsburgh, 24–25 September 2009.

4 In 2009, the G20 membership was Argentina, Australia, Brazil, Canada, China, France, Germany, India, Indonesia, Italy, Japan, Mexico, Russia, Saudi Arabia, South Africa, South Korea, Turkey, the United Kingdom and the United States, as well as the European Union, represented by the rotating council presidency and the European Central Bank.
5 ILO, *Protecting People, Promoting Jobs: From Crisis Response to Recovery and Sustainable Growth*, Communication to G20 leaders by ILO director-general, G20 leaders' meeting, Pittsburgh, 24–25 September 2009.
6 See for example, Somavia's press release following the London G20 summit, "ILO Director-General calls London G20 Summit 'An Important Step Forward on a Difficult Road,'" ILO media release, 3 April 2009.
7 ILO, *Decent Work: Some Strategic Challenges Ahead*, Report of the director-general, International Labour Conference 97th Session, Geneva 2008.
8 ILO, *Tackling the Global Jobs Crisis: Recovery Through Decent Work Policies*, Report of the director-general, International Labour Conference, 98th Session, Geneva 2009.

8 Concluding thoughts: whither the ILO?

1 Peter Waterman, 2005, "From 'Decent Work' to 'The Liberation of Time from Work': Reflections on Work, Emancipation, Utopia and the Global Justice and Solidarity Movement," Inter Activist InfoExchange (available at: http://info.interactivist.net/article.pl?sid=05/03/24/170247); and Peter Waterman, "Needed: A New International Labor Movement for (and against) a Globalised, Networked Capitalism, Global Solidarity Dialogue" (available at: www.antenna.nl/~waterman/needed.html).
2 Guy Standing, "The ILO: An Agency for Globalisation?" *Development and Change* 39, no. 3 (2008): 355–84; Philip Alston and James Heenan, "Shrinking the International Labor Code: An Unintended Consequence of the 1998 ILO Declaration on Fundamental Principles and Rights at Work?" *New York University Journal of International Law and Politics* 36, (2004): 221–64; Philip Alston and James Heenan, "Core Labor Standards and the Transformation of the International Labor Rights Regime," *European Journal of International Law* 15, no. 3 (2004): 457–521; and Philip Alston, "Facing Up to the Complexities of the ILO's Core Labor Standards Agenda," *European Journal of International Law* 16, no. 3 (2005): 467–80.
3 Katherine Hagan, *The International Labor Organisation: Can It Deliver the Social Dimension of Globalization?* Friedrich Ebert Stiftung, Occasional Papers 11, 2003; and Sean Cooney, "Testing Times for the ILO: Institutional Reform for the New International Political Economy," *Comparative Labor Law and Policy Journal* 20 (1999): 365–99. See also, Leah Vosko, "'Decent Work': The Shifting Role of the ILO and the Struggle for Global Social Justice," *Global Social Policy* 2, no. 1 (2002): 19–46; and Elizabeth Prugl, "Global Governance, Women-Friendly: The Promise of the ILO," *Global Social Policy* 2, no. 1 (2002): 9–12.
4 Francis Maupain, "Revitalization Not Retreat: The Real Potential of the 1998 ILO Declaration for the Universal Protection of Workers' Rights," *European Journal of International Law* 16, no. 3 (2005): 439–65; and Brian Langille, "Core Labor Rights, The True Story (Reply to Alston)," *European Journal of International Law* 16, no. 3 (2005): 409–37. See also, Brian Langille.

"The Future of ILO Law, and the ILO," in *The Future of International Law, Proceedings of the American Association of International Law*, 101st Annual Meeting, 2007: 394–96; Brian Langille, "Can We Rely on the ILO?" *Canadian Journal of Labor and Employment Law* 13 (2007): 273–300; and Brian Langille, "The ILO Is Not a State, Its Members Are Not Firms," in G. Politakis, ed., *Protecting Labor Rights as Human Rights: Present and Future of International Supervision* (Geneva: International Labour Office, 2007), 247.

5 Alston and Heenan, "Core Labor Standards and the Transformation of the International Labor Rights Regime," 139.

6 Alston and Heenan, 141.

7 This perspective is developed further in Nigel Haworth and Steve Hughes, "International Political Economy and Industrial Relations," *British Journal of Industrial Relations* 41, no. 4 (2003): 665–82.

Index

Asia 18, 20, 37, 65

Bretton Woods institutions 17, 19, 35, 39, 68, 91, 92; Bretton Woods Accord 16; G20 89; poverty reduction 30; Poverty Reduction Strategy Papers (PRSPs) 30

capitalism 18, 97; Great Depression 11; ILO 43, 97, 99; Social Movement Internationalism school 96–97
child labor: ILO 23, 32, 51; International Program on the Elimination of Child Labor (IPEC) 23, 24; Minimum Age Convention 24, 110; Social Clause 109–10; Worst Forms of Child Labour Convention 24, 26, 110; *see also* human rights; ILO, international labor standards
China 8, 34, 71
civil society 5, 30, 40; fair globalization 38; ILO 41, 100; NGOs 48, 97, 100
Cold War 2, 3, 15–17, 44
competition 10, 18, 38, 62, 67; ILO 95, 97; international 5, 6; US 9
Copenhagen World Summit for Social Development 47, 48, 51, 53, 73–74, 79, 83
corporate social responsibility (CSR) 39, 42, 55, 102
Cox, Robert xvii; International Institute for Labour Studies (IILS) 15

Decent Work 2, 4, 18, 31, 73–79, 90–91; 1998 Declaration 79; assessment 77–78; Decent Work Country Programs (DWCP) 31–32, 77, 78; Decent Work Pilot Programme (DWPP) 77, 111; Decent Work Technical Support Teams (DWTs) 32; employment 30; fair globalization 39, 40; four strategic objectives 74–76, 78, 79, 80; ILO, global economic crisis 90–91, 92, 93; implementation 77; International Monetary Fund (IMF) 30; poverty reduction 30, 77, 78, 91; Poverty Reduction Strategy Papers (PRSPs) 30–31, 77, 78, 111; social dimension of globalization 37; Somavia, Juan 2, 30, 40, 72, 73–79, 80; Strategic Policy Framework 79; World Bank 30; *see also* ILO, technical co-operation; Somavia, Juan
Declaration of Philadelphia 13, 15, 36, 44, 90; 1944 Philadelphia Conference 13; human rights 13; ILO, principles 14, 25, 51, 79, 93, 102–3
Declaration on Fundamental Principles and Rights at Work 2, 3, 45, 46–60, 63, 66–67, 79; 1994 International Labour Conference 36–37, 46, 47; 1998 International Labour Conference 50, 51; assessment 53, 55, 59; conventions/recommendations 50; Copenhagen World Summit for

Social Development 47, 51; core labor standards 24–26, 47–48 (undermined 45); criticism/counterargument 2, 45, 53–60, 79, 97, 109 (critics' alternative 58, 59–60); "follow-up" mechanism 51–53, 70; four fundamental areas of rights 51–52, 63, 67; global governance 47; global regulation 47; globalization 53, 54, 55, 57, 59, 60; Hansenne, Michel 36–37, 46, 47–51, 59, 60, 63, 67–68, 73; ILO renewal 4, 33, 36–37, 48, 50, 60, 63, 72, 73; market fundamentalism 54, 55, 59; rationale 47–48, 53, 59; rights/principles debate 54, 56, 57–58, 59, 79; social dimension of globalization 37, 41, 48, 67–68; soft law/binding law 45, 46, 53, 54, 58, 66–67, 68; Somavia, Juan 46, 52, 60, 74, 80; standard-setting 45, 46, 47–50, 53–56, 58, 59; supporters 46–47, 53, 57, 63, 70; targeted standards 48–50; *see also* fair globalization; Hansenne, Michel; ILO, assessment/criticisms; ILO, globalization; ILO, international labor standards

democracy: fair globalization 38; ILO xvii; labor standards 13; "modern" social democracy 34, 108; neo-liberalism 108

developing countries: fair globalization 38; global economic crisis 86, 87, 88, 89, 91; ILO 14, 15, 16–17; Multilateral Organisation Performance Assessment Network (MOPAN) 31; New International Economic Order 16; Social Clause 62; Somavia, Juan 83

development 29–31, 68, 75; Copenhagen World Summit for Social Development 47, 48, 51, 53, 73–74, 79, 83; ILO, aims 17, 31, 75; International Development Associations (IDA) 30; Millennium Development Goals (MDGs) 31; social development 15, 21, 51, 68; Somavia, Juan 83; UK Department for International Development (DFID) 29; *see also* Decent Work

discrimination 25, 26, 32, 51, 109

economic crisis 1; 1990 economic crisis 65; 2007 global economic crisis 1, 4, 30, 85–86 (beginning 85; severity 85–86); Great Depression 8, 9–11, 40, 85–86, 94; interventionism 1, 88, 90, 91, 93; *see also* ILO, global economic crisis

economics: economic, financial, social policy interplay 10, 12, 88–89; global production systems 38, 41; ILO 5, 6, 18, 23–24; informal economy 16, 35, 87; international financial system 38; market fundamentalism 33–36, 38, 39–40, 44, 62, 108; New International Economic Order 16; policy 33–34; United Kingdom 17; US 17; Washington Consensus 19, 33–34, 108; *see also* economic crisis; G20; globalization; ILO, global economic crisis; ILO, globalization; liberalism; market; trade

employer: 1998 Declaration 46, 63; ILO's tripartite structure 3, 5, 7, 23, 60, 99 (labor standards 70)

employment: fair globalization 38, 41; GDP/unemployment relationship 86–87; global economic crisis 86–87, 88, 90, 92 (women 86; young people 86); Great Depression 9–11; ILO, aims 21, 30, 75, 80, 90, 93; OLI, Global Jobs Pact 90–93; market fundamentalism 34; unemployment 10, 16, 17, 34 (communism 10–11; fascism 11); World Employment Programme (WEP) 35; *see also* Decent Work; ILO, global economic crisis; labor market

European Union 62, 66, 86, 89

fair globalization 1, 36–43, 74, 79–80; 2008 Declaration on Social

Justice for a Fair Globalisation 37, 74, 79–80, 92, 112 (1998 Declaration 80; supreme statement of ILO principles/values 79); accountability of institutions 37, 39, 41; Decent Work 80; *A Fair Globalisation* report 37–45, 46, 74, 79, 82 (follow-up 74); global governance xvi, 2, 37, 38, 40, 41, 42–43; international policies 37, 38–39; mobilizing for change 37, 39, 41; national governance 37, 38, 40–41; social dimension of globalization 1, 19, 35, 36–37, 39, 41, 42; Somavia, Juan 1, 40–45, 46, 74, 79–80; Strategic Policy Framework 80; sustainable globalization 38, 39, 40, 41; Working Party on the Social Dimensions of Globalisation 74, 79, 112; World Commission on the Social Dimensions of Globalisation 37–45, 68; *see also* globalization; ILO, globalization; Somavia, Juan

Financial Stability Board 1, 88
forced labor 26, 51, 73, 109; Burma 70–71; *see also* human rights; ILO, international labor standards

G20 86, 88–90; 2009 G8+6 Labor and Employment Ministers' Meeting 92; 2009 London Summit 1, 86, 89, 92; 2009 Pittsburgh Summit 86, 88–89; Bretton Woods institutions 89; GDP 89; global economic management 88, 89; Global Plan for Recovery and Reform 86; ILO and the G20 in 2009 86, 88–90, 92; membership 88, 89, 113 ("BRIC" countries 89); response to the crisis 88–89; role 88; *see also* ILO, global economic crisis
General Agreement on Tariffs and Trade (GATT) 61, 62, 64, 69; labor standards 62; Uruguay Round 1–2, 18, 61, 62, 64; US 62, 64; *see also* Social Clause
global governance: 1998 Declaration 47; Decent Work 40; fair globalization 30, 37, 38, 40, 41, 42–43; Hansenne, Michel 30, 72, 102; ILO xvi, 2, 37, 38, 40, 41, 42–43, 101–3 (tripartism 103); Somavia, Juan 30, 40, 41, 102; *see also* fair globalization
globalization 18–19, 33; labor standards 3–4; "modern" social democracy 34, 108; neo-liberalism 33, 108; notion 108; social dimension 1, 19, 35, 36–37, 39, 41, 42; sustainable globalization 38, 39, 40, 41; Washington Consensus 33–34, 108; *see also* fair globalization; ILO, globalization
government: global economic crisis 1; ILO's tripartite structure 3, 5, 7, 23, 44 (labor standards 70); market fundamentalism 44; "naming and shaming" 71, 111

Hansenne, Michel 2, 6, 17, 19, 33; 1994 International Labour Conference 36–37, 46, 47, 65, 67; 1998 Declaration 36–37, 46, 47–51, 59, 60, 63, 67, 73; global governance 30, 72, 102; ILO, enforcement 71, 111; ILO, globalization 36–37, 44, 46, 65, 67–68; ILO renewal 2, 4, 33, 36–37, 48, 50, 60, 63, 72, 73, 83, 84, 89, 94; multilateral trade system 67; Social Clause 62, 63, 65, 67–68, 69–70, 72; *see also* ILO, directors-general; ILO, history; Somavia, Juan
human rights: fair globalization 39; ILO, aims 13, 15, 17, 20, 23–24, 38; *see also* child labor; forced labor; ILO, international labor standards

ILO, accountability xvii, 41, 74, 100; corporate social responsibility (CSR) 39; fair globalization 37, 39, 41; *see also* ILO, assessment/criticisms
ILO, aims xvi, 1, 5–6, 14, 21, 32, 36, 51, 67, 74–75, 84; development 17, 31, 75; employment 21, 30, 74–75,

78, 80, 81, 90, 93; four strategic objectives 21, 30, 74–76, 77, 78, 79, 81; human rights 13, 15, 17, 20, 23–24, 38; labor standards 3, 5, 6, 17, 21, 23, 30, 32, 66, 75, 78, 80, 81, 90, 98–99, 101–3; main concerns 5, 6; poverty reduction 17, 29–30, 41, 77, 78; social dialogue 21, 23, 30, 39, 75, 78, 80, 81, 93; social protection 21, 29, 30, 41, 42, 68, 75, 78, 80, 81, 93, 102; Somavia, Juan 74–75, 76, 77, 78, 80, 81; Strategic Policy Framework 81; *see also* child labor; Decent Work; Declaration of Philadelphia; Declaration on Fundamental Principles and Rights at Work; ILO, globalization; ILO, international labor standards; ILO, role

ILO, assessment/criticisms 2–3, 4, 30, 83, 95–103; 1998 Declaration 2, 45, 53–60, 79, 97, 109; Alston, Philip 45, 57–58, 79, 96, 97, 98–99, 109; Cooney, Sean 96, 99–100; Hagen, Katherine 96, 99, 100; Hansenne, Michel 77; Heenan, James 45, 96, 97, 98–99, 109; ILO and the International Labor Standards Regime 101–3; ILO school 96, 101; Langille, Brian 57–58, 79, 83, 96, 101, 109; Maupain, Francis 55–56, 96, 101, 109; Organizational Challenges school 96, 99–101; post-1994 model 83, 89, 97–102, 105; Social Movement Internationalism school 96–97, 102; Somavia, Juan 42, 76–77, 80, 83, 91, 96, 101; Soviet Union 15; Standing, Guy 82, 96, 97–98, 99, 100 (1998 Declaration 45, 54–55, 57, 109; globalization 35, 43; Somavia, Juan 82); Strategic Misdirection school 96, 97–99; success 5, 58, 69, 78, 95, 101, 102; Waterman, Peter 96–97, 98

ILO, conferences 7, 12, 16, 23, 30; International Labour Conference 9, 12, 23, 24, 36, 107 (1941 New York Conference 12; 1944 Philadelphia Conference 13; 1994 International Labour Conference 36–37, 46, 47, 65, 67; 1998 International Labour Conference 50, 51; 1999 International Labour Conference 74; 2008 International Labour Conference 79, 90; 2009 International Labour Conference 90; enforcement 70–71, 111); World Employment Conference 17

ILO, conventions/recommendations xvi, 24–27, 48, 50, 79; 1998 Declaration 50; Committee of Experts on the Application of Conventions and Recommendations 27, 28, 70, 111; Commission of Inquiry 28, 29, 70; Conference Committee on the Application of Conventions and Recommendations 70, 111; core conventions 24–25, 62, 109–10; core labor standards 18, 24–26, 38, 48, 62, 64, 65, 69, 73, 98, 100; freedom of association 15, 18, 24–25, 28–29, 46, 51, 56, 109; Hansenne, Michel 50; Minimum Age Convention 24, 110; right to collective bargaining 15, 18, 25, 51 (Right to Organise and Collective Bargaining 24); supervisory mechanisms 27; trade unions 18; US 25–27, 70; Worst Forms of Child Labour Convention 24, 26, 110; *see also* Declaration on Fundamental Principles and Rights at Work; ILO, international labor standards

ILO, directors-general 2, 5–6, 19, 20, 21, 32; Blanchard, Francis 16–17, 18, 19, 33; Butler, Harold 6, 7, 8, 9, 10, 11; Jenks, Wilfred 15–16; Morse, David 14–15, 17; Phelan, Edward 12–13, 15; Thomas, Albert 6–7, 8–9, 16, 20, 32, 74; Winant, John G. 11–12, 15; *see also* Hansenne, Michel; Somavia, Juan

ILO, enforcement 27, 58, 63, 70–71, 95–96, 100, 111; 1998

Declaration, "follow-up" mechanism 51–53, 70; Burma 70–71; China 71; Commission of Inquiry 28, 29, 70; Committee of Experts on the Application of Conventions and Recommendations 27, 28, 70, 111; Conference Committee on the Application of Conventions and Recommendations 70, 111; Hansenne, Michel 71, 111; moral suasion 63, 69, 70, 71, 95; "naming and shaming" 28, 56, 71, 95, 111; Social Clause 69, 70–71; soft law/binding law 45, 46, 53, 54, 58, 66–67, 68; supervisory mechanisms 27–29, 70

ILO, global economic crisis 4, 30, 85–94; 2007 global economic crisis 1, 4, 30, 85–86; Bretton Woods institutions 89, 91, 92; Decent Work 90–91, 92, 93; developed countries 85, 86, 88; developing countries 86, 87, 88, 89, 91; employment 86–87, 88, 90, 92; G20 86, 88–90; GDP 86–87, 89; GDP/unemployment relationship 86–87; ILO and the G20 86, 88–90, 92; ILO, Global Jobs Pact 90–93 (assessment 93; Global Employment Agenda 90; key dimensions 92–93; rationale 92); ILO's report 86–88, 89; interventions 88, 90, 91, 93; poverty 87, 88; recovery 88, 91, 92; social welfare 87, 88, 90; Somavia, Juan 86, 89, 90–94; UN 87, 91, 92; US 85, 89; World Bank 85–86; *see also* economic crisis; G20; Somavia, Juan

ILO, globalization 3–4, 18–19, 32, 33–45; 1998 Declaration 53, 54, 55, 57, 59, 60; capability development 42; challenge of globalization 36, 43–44, 59, 65, 73; Decent Work 39, 40, 74; fair globalization 36–43; Hansenne, Michel 36–37, 44, 46, 65, 67–68; ILO, global regulation 35, 36, 40, 47, 95; market fundamentalism 33–36, 38, 39–40, 44, 108; social dimension 1, 19, 35, 36–37, 39, 41, 42, 48, 67–68, 112 (sustainable social dimension 41, 42); Somavia, Juan 36, 40–45, 46, 72; sustainable globalization 38, 39, 40, 41; tripartism 34–35, 40, 41, 44; Washington Consensus 19, 33–34, 108; *see also* Declaration on Fundamental Principles and Rights at Work; fair globalization; Somavia, Juan

ILO, Governing Body 7, 10, 11, 12, 21; 1998 Declaration 52, 53; supervisory mechanisms 27–28; tripartite structure 23; *see also* ILO, structure/organization

ILO, history xvi-xvii, 2–3, 5–19; Cold War 2, 3, 15–16, 44; Eurocentrism 7, 11, 14; ILO renewal 78–79, 93 (Hansenne, Michel 2, 4, 33, 36–37, 48, 50, 60, 63, 72, 73, 83, 84, 89, 94; Somavia, Juan 60, 80, 81–82, 83–84, 89, 94); inter-war period 8–14, 35, 36, 40, 87; League of Nations (LON) xvii, 3, 8–9, 10, 14, 19, 94, 95, 103; Nobel Peace Prize xvi, 3, 15, 35; origins 5; post-1994 model 79, 83, 89, 93, 97–102, 105; post-war period 14–18, 19, 94; recent period 18–19, 32, 35–36, 44; struggle for institutional life 6–8; UN system 13, 14, 68; US membership and involvement 7, 10–14, 107; *see also* Declaration on Fundamental Principles and Rights at Work; Hansenne, Michel; ILO, directors-general; Social Clause; Somavia, Juan; United States

ILO, impact xvi, 3; 1998 Declaration 47, 48, 52–53, 54, 57, 79; Decent Work 78, 92; *see also* ILO, assessment/criticisms

ILO, international labor standards 3, 9–10, 13, 15, 17–18, 21, 23–27, 32, 84, 89–90, 98; 1998 Declaration 24–26, 45, 46, 47–50, 53–56, 58, 59; core labor standards 18, 24–26,

38, 48, 62, 64, 65, 69, 73, 98, 100 (and trade 66; fair globalization 38; Social Clause 62, 69; undermined 45); cross-border movement of people 38, 41; global governance 41; ILO, aim 3, 5, 6, 17, 21, 23, 30, 32, 66, 75, 78, 80, 81, 90, 98–99, 101–3; ILO as center of global labor standards process 60; International Labor Code 24, 27; International Labor Standards Regime 101–3; social dimension of globalization 37; standard-setting 9–10, 11, 14, 15, 20, 45, 46, 47–50, 52, 53–56, 58, 59, 63, 69, 75, 78, 79, 80, 89–90, 103; targeted standards 48–50; trade/labor standards link 3–4, 17–18, 54, 60, 62–65, 68, 72; *see also* Declaration on Fundamental Principles and Rights at Work; ILO, aims; ILO, conventions/recommendations; ILO, enforcement; ILO, role; Social Clause

ILO, membership 14, 21; Declaration of Philadelphia 13, 14, 25, 51; expansion 14, 15, 20; Soviet Union 9, 15, 16, 43; US 2, 7, 10–14, 16, 17, 25–27, 35, 44, 107, 108

ILO, policy 6, 10, 20, 77, 83, 90, 94, 101; macroeconomic policy 42, 75; Policy Coherence Initiative (PCI) 39, 68; policy co-ordination 2, 42, 91; Strategic Policy Framework 79, 80, 81; *see also* Decent Work; ILO, social policy

ILO, politics xvi, 7, 13–14, 82–83, 92, 93, 99; Cold War 2, 15–17; *see also* Declaration on Fundamental Principles and Rights at Work; Social Clause

ILO, research xvii, 42, 81; academics xvii, 41; conventions, recommendations 24; International Institute for Labour Studies (IILS) 15, 20; International Labour Office 21; poverty reduction 30

ILO, role 1, 7, 12, 13, 15, 41, 57, 59, 66, 69, 73, 78, 80, 87, 90–91, 93, 103; globalization 43; ILO, global economic crisis 30, 87, 89–90, 91, 93, 94; international role 30, 33, 72, 103; post-war world 12, 14, 19; social development 21; social protection 24, 29, 38, 39, 67, 90, 102; standard-setting 9–10, 11, 14, 15, 20, 45, 46, 47–50, 52, 53–56, 58, 59, 63, 69, 75, 78, 79, 80, 89–90, 103; *see also* ILO aims; ILO, international labor standards; ILO, technical co-operation

ILO, social policy 20, 30, 75; economic, financial, social policy interplay 10, 12, 88–89; ILO, social dialogue 21, 23, 30, 39, 75, 77, 78, 79, 81, 82, 91, 93; ILO, social justice 2, 5, 7, 10, 15, 30, 54, 63, 80, 83, 84, 99, 101; ILO, social protection 21, 29, 30, 41, 42, 68, 75, 78, 81, 93, 102; social dimension of globalization 1, 19, 35, 36–37, 39, 41, 42; *see also* Decent Work; Declaration on Fundamental Principles and Rights at Work; fair globalization; ILO, policy

ILO, structure/organization 3, 20–32; budget 12, 17, 21, 29, 78–79, 80, 81, 82; constitution 12, 13, 25, 28, 51, 70; criticism 82; governance 20–21, 32; Governing Body 7, 10, 11, 12, 21, 23, 27–28, 52, 53; headquarters 3 (Geneva 3, 12, 14, 21, 23, 32, 65; Montreal 12, 13, 15); independence 8, 10, 93; International Labor Code 24, 27; International Labour Office 3, 21, 22, 32; Multilateral Organisation Performance Assessment Network 31–32; regional offices 15, 20, 23, 29, 31, 32; States of Chief Industrial Importance 23; supervisory mechanisms 27–29; tripartism xvi, xvii, 3, 5, 9, 16, 20, 21–23, 29, 32, 50, 93, 99, 103 (ILO, globalization 34–35, 40, 41, 43, 44; labor standards 70;

Somavia, Juan 40, 41, 80, 81); UN system 13, 21, 43; *see also* ILO, conferences; ILO directors-general
ILO, technical co-operation 23, 29–31, 71, 81; capacity building 29, 42–43, 75, 77, 78; Decent Work 29–31, 75, 77, 78; International Training Centre 15, 20–21, 41; Latin America 12; poverty reduction 29; Poverty Reduction Strategy Papers (PRSPs) 30–31; technical assistance program 14–15, 17, 29; training 14, 20–21, 29; *see also* Decent Work
International Court of Justice 28, 70–71
international institutions 12, 14, 21, 30, 39, 40, 90, 91, 95; ILO, institutional linkage 66, 67, 68, 72, 74, 84, 86, 89–90, 91, 93, 94; *see also* Somavia, Juan
International Monetary Fund (IMF) 1, 17, 72; IMF/ILO relation 2, 17, 29–30; poverty reduction 29–30; Poverty Reduction and Growth Facility (PRGF) 30; Washington Consensus 33–34, 108

labor legislation 5, 6, 7, 29, 73; *see also* Decent Work; Declaration of Philadelphia; Declaration on Fundamental Principles and Rights at Work; ILO, conventions/ recommendations; ILO, international labor standards
labor market 42, 66, 95; flexibility 2, 44; global economic crisis 86–88, 91, 92; *see also* employment
labor standards: China 71; fair globalization 38; globalization 3–4; national labor standards 7; trade/labor standards link 3–4, 17–18, 54, 60, 62–65, 68, 72; US 9; *see also* ILO, conventions/ recommendations; ILO, enforcement; ILO, international labor standards; Social Clause
Latin America 12, 20
League of Nations (LON) xvii, 3, 10, 14, 19, 94, 95, 103; decline 8–9

liberalism 1, 11, 14, 17; globalization 34; Great Depression 11; market 1, 17; neo-liberalism 33, 57, 87, 97–98, 108; unemployment 11; *see also* capitalism; market; trade

market 48; globalization 43–44; market fundamentalism 33–36, 38, 39–40, 44, 62, 108 (1998 Declaration 54, 55, 59; economics 33–34; Social Clause 62; social policy 34, 35); market liberalism 1, 17–18; *see also* economics; globalization; ILO, globalization; liberalism; trade

national governance: fair globalization 37, 38, 40–41
North American Free Trade Agreement (NAFTA) 62; North American Agreement on Labor Cooperation (NAALC) 62

Organisation for Economic Co-operation and Development (OECD) 25, 48, 85

politics: anti-imperialism 10–11; Cold War 2, 3, 15–17, 44; communism 10–11, 13–14; fascism 11; ILO, politics xvi, 2, 7, 13–14, 15–17, 82–83, 92, 93, 99; inter-war period 8
poverty reduction 18, 29–30, 41; ILO 17, 29–30, 41, 77, 78; International Monetary Fund (IMF) 29–30; Poverty Reduction Strategy Papers (PRSPs) 30; World Bank 29–30
protectionism 52, 62, 63, 65, 66, 67, 97–98

regulation 1, 98; 1998 Declaration 47; global regulation 35, 40, 47, 95; ILO, globalization 35, 36, 40, 47, 95; interventionism 1, 88, 90, 91, 93; Social Clause 25, 62, 64, 70 (Clinton, Bill 65–66); *see also* economic crisis; ILO, global economic crisis

Social Clause 2, 24, 57, 61–72; 1998 Declaration 63, 66–68, 70; brief history 64–66 (generic proposal 62); conventions/recommendations 63; core conventions 62, 70, 109–10; core standards 61, 62, 64, 65, 66, 69; distancing the Social Clause model 68–70, 110; European Union 62, 66; GATT 61, 62, 64, 69; General System of Preferences (GSP) 62; Hansenne, Michel 62, 63, 65, 67–68, 69–70, 72; ILO 66–70, 72, 110 (Policy Coherence Initiative (PCI) 68); a polarized debate 62–63; protectionism 62, 63, 65, 66; Social Clause, ILO and enforcement 69, 70–71; Somavia, Juan 65, 66, 68, 72, 111; standard-setting 63, 69; trade/labor standards link 3–4, 17–18, 54, 60, 62–65, 68, 72; trade union 62, 63; US 25, 62, 64, 65–66, 70; where to after the Social Clause? 71–72; WTO 60, 62, 64–66, 69, 72; WTO/ILO collaboration 63–64, 66, 68, 69, 110 (2007 Joint ILO/WTO Report on Trade and Employment 68); *see also* ILO, history; ILO, international labor standards; World Trade Organization (WTO)

social policy *see* ILO, social policy

Somavia, Juan 2, 6, 17, 73–84, 111; 1998 Declaration 46, 52, 60, 74, 80; capability development 42–43; Copenhagen World Summit for Social Development 47, 73–74, 79, 83; criticism 82, 83, 84, 111; Decent Work 2, 30, 40, 72, 73–79, 80, 90–91, 93, 111; fair globalization 1, 40–45, 46, 74, 79–80; *A Fair Globalisation* report 40–45, 74, 79, 82 (follow-up 74); global governance 30, 40, 41, 102; Global Jobs Pact 90–93; ILO, accountability 74; ILO, assessment 42, 76–77, 80, 83, 91; ILO, global economic crisis 86, 89, 90–94; ILO, globalization 36, 40–45, 46, 72; ILO, institutional linkage 66, 67, 68, 72, 74, 84, 86, 89–90, 91, 93, 94; ILO, reform 60, 80, 81–82, 83–84, 89, 94; ILO, tripartism 40, 41, 80, 81; legacy 83–84; poverty reduction 30, 41; Social Clause 65, 66, 68, 72, 111; strategic planning/performance 74, 80–83, 111; Strategic Policy Framework 79, 80, 81; sustainable social dimension 41, 42; *see also* Decent Work; fair globalization; Hansenne, Michel; ILO, directors-general; ILO, history

Soviet Union 34; Great Depression 10–11; ILO 9, 14, 15, 16, 43

trade: competition 9; fair globalization 38, 67; free trade 34, 38, 61; global 16; global economic crisis 86, 89; international trade 6, 14, 48; liberalization 33, 67–68; North American Free Trade Agreement (NAFTA) 62; trade/labor standards link 3–4, 17–18, 23, 37, 54, 60, 62–65, 68, 72; *see also* economics; globalization; ILO, globalization; liberalism; Social Clause; trade; World Trade Organization (WTO)

trade union: freedom of association 15, 18, 24–25, 28–29, 46, 51, 56, 109 (Committee on Freedom of Association 28, 46; Fact-Finding and Conciliation Commission on Freedom of Association 28–29; Freedom of Association and Protection of the Right to Organise 24); ILO's tripartite structure 3, 5, 7, 23, 34–35, 44, 60, 97, 99 (labor standards 70); International Confederation of Free Trade Unions (ICFTU) 63; International Trade Union Federation 7, 96; market fundamentalism 34–35, 44; post-war trade unionism 16, 17; Social Clause 62, 63; Social Movement Internationalism school 96–97; World Federation of Trade Unions (WFTU) 14

unemployment *see* employment
United Kingdom: Department for International Development (DFID) 29; Poverty Reduction Strategy Papers (PRSPs) 30–31; Thatcher, Margaret 17
United Nations: global economic crisis 87, 91, 92; ILO 13, 14, 68; ILO/UNDP Memorandum of Understanding 68; Millennium Development Goals (MDGs) 31, 68; New International Economic Order 16; poverty reduction 29–30; UN Economic and Social Council (ECOSOC) 29; UN Global Compact 64; UN Security Council 106; *see also* League of Nations
United States 8; Clinton, Bill 65–66; global economic crisis 85, 89; globalization 34; Great Depression 9; ILO, membership 7, 10–14, 107 (conventions ratification 25–27; withdrawal/return 2, 16, 17, 35, 44, 107, 108); isolationism 9, 12, 13; League of Nations 9, 11–12; Perkins, Francis 9, 107; Reagan, Ronald 17; Roosevelt, Franklin D. 9, 11–12; Social Clause 25, 62, 64, 70; trade/labor standards link 62; Truman, Harry S. 14

war: First World War 5, 7, 13; labor legislation 5, 7; Second World War 3, 13, 14, 95; Sino-Japanese War 8
Washington Consensus 17, 19, 33–34, 108
World Bank 17, 72; global economic crisis 85–86; International Development Associations (IDA) 30; poverty reduction 29–30; Washington Consensus 33–34, 108; World Bank/ILO relation 17, 29–30
World Trade Organization (WTO) 1–2, 24, 48, 62; Doha meeting 66; fair globalization 38; Geneva meeting 65; regulation 35; Seattle meeting 65–66; Singapore meeting 64–65; Social Clause 60, 62, 64–66, 69, 72; WTO/ILO collaboration 63–64, 66, 68, 69, 110 (2007 Joint ILO/WTO Report on Trade and Employment 68); *see also* Social Clause; trade